THE PLAIN-ENGLISH GUIDE TO OFAC ECONOMIC SANCTIONS FOR FOREIGN COMPANIES

By Heidi Hunter

St. Paul, Minnesota

The Plain-English Guide to Economic Sanctions for Foreign Companies

Copyright © 2024, 2005 Heidi Hunter

First Edition: December 2024
Second Edition: April 2025

All rights reserved. No part of this book may be reproduced in any form or by any electronic or mechanical means, including information storage and retrieval systems, without permission in writing from the publisher, except by reviewers, who may quote brief passages in a review. The author expressly prohibits any entity from using this publication to train artificial intelligence (AI) technologies to generate text, including, without limitation, technologies capable of generating works in the same style or genre as this publication. The author reserves all rights to license the use of this work for generative AI training and development of machine learning language models.

Published by LilAbby Press
St. Paul, Minnesota

ISBN: 979-8-9921409-9-6 (paperback)

cover design by Heidi Hunter

TABLE OF CONTENTS

Disclaimer 1

Introduction 2

Definitions 3

1 Introduction to Economic Sanctions 10

2 Types of Sanctions 14

3 Who Has To Comply with US Economic Sanctions? 20

4 Other Nuances about OFAC Sanctions 24

5 Trade Sanctions 30

6 How Economic Sanctions Affect Your Company 33

7 How Do I Comply with OFAC Sanctions? 36

8 Scanning/Screening 42

9 What if My Customer Is Sanctioned? 48

10 Can I Do Any Business with Sanctioned Parties or Countries? 52

11 Legal Considerations 57

12 Managing US Parent Versus Foreign Branch or Subsidiary Conflicts 61

13 Penalties for Non-Compliance 64

14 Conclusion 66

15 Test Your Knowledge 67

References 72

Author Biography 74

All Books in the Plain-English Guide Series by Heidi Hunter 75

Notes 65

Disclaimer

The information provided in this book is for informational purposes only and is not intended to constitute legal advice. The author of this book is not an attorney, is not providing legal advice, and is not creating an attorney-client relationship with the reader.

Readers should not act or rely on any information in this book without seeking the advice of a lawyer. Any reliance upon the information contained in this guide is solely at the reader's own risk.

The author makes no representations or warranties about the completeness, accuracy, reliability, or suitability of the information in this book.

While every effort has been made to provide accurate and complete guidance, it's critical to understand that this guide does not guarantee an effective sanctions compliance program free from fines or penalties. Compliance with economic sanctions regulations is a complex and evolving area, and the effectiveness of any program depends on various factors, including the specific circumstances of the reader's business and the actions of relevant regulatory authorities. Therefore, the author cannot guarantee specific outcomes or results from implementing the suggestions provided in this guide. This information is a tool to develop and enhance your sanctions compliance program, but the ultimate responsibility for compliance rests with the reader and their organization.

In no event shall the author be liable for any loss or damage whatsoever arising from, or in connection with, the use of the information contained in this book.

Introduction

Economic sanctions are powerful tools governments and international bodies use to influence the behavior of nations, businesses, and individuals. Navigating the complexities of sanctions can be difficult for Americans, let alone foreign companies that don't regularly deal with US sanctions.

Understanding and managing the risks associated with sanctions is crucial for compliance and avoiding severe penalties. Civil and criminal fines can reach millions of dollars and generate negative publicity, harming your company's reputation with customers and business partners.

Sanctions compliance isn't just about avoiding fines, however. It's also about upholding legal and ethical standards, protecting your company's reputation, and staying competitive in a global market.

This guide focuses on sanctions issues foreign companies face when doing business with the US. It explains US sanctions, their impact on foreign organizations, and steps companies can take to remain compliant.

Whether you're a sanctions professional, new to the field, or need a basic understanding of key sanctions concepts, this guide provides clear insights to help you navigate compliance challenges.

We'll primarily focus on economic sanctions enforced by the Office of Foreign Assets Control (OFAC), with some discussion of trade sanctions managed by the Department of State and the Bureau of Industry and Security. We'll also compare OFAC sanctions with those from major economies like the UK and the EU.

Several examples of foreign companies penalized by OFAC are included to highlight the importance of following the key concepts in this guide. These examples can help you explain to management why complying with US sanctions is essential, especially if there's resistance within your company.

Definitions

Some of the terms referenced in this guide are defined below.

Beneficial Owner

The person who ultimately owns, benefits from, or controls an asset.

Blocking Program

An OFAC sanctions program that requires a sanctioned party's assets to be blocked or frozen. US persons are prohibited from doing business with them.

Bureau of Industry and Security (BIS)

The US Department of Commerce's Bureau of Industry and Security (BIS) administers and enforces export controls on dual-use and certain munitions items.

Business Partner

Any third party you do business with. A business partner can be a vendor, a subcontractor, an attorney, a joint venture partner, a consultant, or an agent and representative acting on a company's behalf.

Claimant

The person or entity that requests payment from an insurance company for a loss covered by a policy. The claimant could be the named insured, or it could be a third party seeking compensation.

Comprehensive Sanctions

A trade embargo against a country. Most transactions are prohibited. Countries under comprehensive sanctions are Iran, Cuba, Syria[1], North Korea, and Russian-held areas of Ukraine, such as Crimea.

Correspondent Banking

A US financial institution acts as a middleman for a foreign financial institution, giving them access to the US banking system through a single account. Generally, a foreign bank will conduct all customer transactions through this account.

Debt/Equity Restrictions

OFAC restricts the issuance of long-term debt (with terms over fourteen or thirty days, for example) or the purchase of equity for some non-SDN parties. "Debt" includes bonds, loans, extensions of credit, loan guarantees, letters of credit, discount notes or bills, or commercial paper, while equity includes stocks and shares.[2]

Department of State (DoS)

The Department of State has several divisions that oversee the export of defense-related items and services and weapons of mass destruction.

Directive

A Directive is a determination by the President that certain activity is prohibited under an Executive Order. There might be limits on debt or equity, import/export restrictions, or restrictions on specific sectors such as energy, defense, and finance.

Economic Sanctions

The government's restrictions or penalties on individuals, entities, groups, governments, or countries to achieve particular foreign policy or national security goals.

Environmental Scanning

Also known as e-scanning. Environmental scanning is how you, as the sanctions compliance professional, stay updated on changes in economic sanctions regulations.

Executive Order

When the President wants to impose new economic sanctions, he will issue an Executive Order. The Executive Order explains why sanctions are needed, the laws under which the Executive Order is created, and who can be sanctioned under the program.

Facilitation

Assisting others in conducting a transaction that violates sanctions if you had conducted it yourself.

Freezing or Blocking Assets

Preventing a sanctioned party from accessing or using assets you hold that belong to them, such as a bank account or an insurance claim. Assets are deposited into a blocked bank account when possible.

Foreign Company

In this guide, a foreign company refers to any entity neither located in nor registered to do business in the United States.

Indirect

Selling goods or services to someone acting on behalf of a sanctioned party or country.

Internal Controls

Internal controls are the processes, procedures, and measures that prevent and detect sanctions violations.

List-Based Sanctions

Programs where sanctioned parties are added to the Specially Designated Nationals (SDN) list. Most transactions with them are prohibited, and assets you hold that belong to them may need to be blocked.

Nexus

Transactions connected to the US, such as participation by a US party, sale of a US good or service, and transacting in US dollars or through the US financial system. Non-US persons carrying out a transaction outside the US may be required to comply with US sanctions if that transaction has a US nexus.

The term is also used when referencing whether a particular transaction or payment has a connection to a sanctioned country, party, or good.

Office of Foreign Assets Control (OFAC)

The Office of Foreign Assets Control (OFAC), part of the US Department of the Treasury, oversees most US sanctions programs.

OFAC Regulations

OFAC incorporates sanctions laws and executive orders into its own regulations for a program, which are issued in the Code of Federal Regulations (CFR). The CFR is where all rules implemented by the Federal government are published.

OFAC Sanctions

Sanctions administered by the Office of Foreign Assets Control (OFAC). You'll see terms like "economic sanctions," "OFAC sanctions," "trade sanctions," "sanctions regulations," "OFAC regulations," and "US sanctions" used interchangeably in this guide.

Possible Match/False Positive/Positive Match

A possible match occurs when your sanctions screening system determines that your customer may be a match to a person on the SDN list. A possible or potential match is also known as an "alert" or a "hit." A positive match, on the other hand, is a possible match that is determined to be an actual match once your customer's information is compared to the sanctioned party's information.

Risk Assessment

A risk assessment is a method for identifying, analyzing, and addressing a company's sanctions risks. It helps pinpoint any weaknesses in the program and lays out a plan to fix them.

Sanctions Compliance Officer (SCO)

The person within an organization with ultimate responsibility for the sanctions compliance program.

Sanctions Compliance Program (SCP)

The policies, procedures, and controls that help a company comply with sanctions regulations.

Sanctions Compliance/Sanctions Compliance Team

Sanctions compliance is the function within a company responsible for managing the policy, program, and controls related to sanctions compliance. The SCO is part of this function. This function may also include a separate team dedicated to sanctions (i.e., the Sanctions Compliance Team).

Sanctions Evasion

Sanctions evasion occurs when people try to structure a transaction to get around sanctions.

Sanctions Program

A sanctions program consists of all the laws, Executive Orders, OFAC regulations, guidance, licenses, and FAQs related to restrictions against a specific country or activity. It governs what you can and cannot do.

Sanctions Risk

Sanctions risk refers to potential threats or weaknesses that, if not adequately managed by internal controls, can result in violations of OFAC's regulations.

Scanning/Screening

Reviewing a customer or transaction to see if there is a potential sanctions issue. This can involve scanning a name against OFAC's watchlists or reviewing a transaction for a sanctions nexus.

Secondary Sanctions

Also known as "extraterritorial sanctions." Under certain programs, like those related to Iran or Russia, non-US persons can face penalties under US law for prohibited activities, even if they have no ties, connection, or nexus to the US. Additionally, US entities will be prohibited from engaging in transactions with these penalized parties.

Sectoral Sanctions

Sectoral sanctions prohibit certain activities in targeted industries with designated entities, while any other activity is legal.

Specially Designated National (SDN)/Sanctioned Party

An individual, company, organization, group, government, vessel, or aircraft sanctioned by OFAC and listed on the Specially Designated Nationals (SDN) list. Their assets are blocked, and US persons are generally prohibited from dealing with them.[3]

The 50 Percent Rule

Entities majority-owned (50 percent or more) by one or more blocked persons, either through direct or indirect ownership, are also considered sanctioned despite not being named on a watchlist.

US-Origin Goods

A good is considered of US origin if it is "all or virtually all" made in the United States. The origin refers to where the product was produced or manufactured, not where it was shipped from. Goods located in or passing through the US are also considered US origin. Foreign-made goods containing at least 25 percent US-origin content (10 percent for certain countries) or those directly made from US technology or software are also classified as US origin.

US Person

US citizens anywhere in the world, US-incorporated businesses, including their foreign branches, people who are in the US for any reason, even if they are citizens of another country, and any persons transacting in the US financial system, US dollars, or US goods.

Watchlists

Watchlists are lists maintained by OFAC of sanctioned parties. These lists can be Specially Designated Nationals (SDN) and non-SDN lists. These lists specify various prohibitions, from full asset blocking and transaction bans (for those on the SDN lists) to targeted restrictions (for those on the non-SDN lists).

1
Introduction to Economic Sanctions

At its simplest, economic sanctions mean you are not allowed to do business with certain countries or parties. Before proceeding with any business transactions, you must do your homework to identify any potential sanctions issues.

This chapter will explain economic sanctions, why they are used, and which US government agency is in charge of implementing and enforcing them.

What Are Sanctions?

Sanctions are restrictions or penalties the government imposes on countries, people, groups, governments, or industries to help achieve certain goals in foreign policy and national security. For example, the United States may prohibit US citizens from engaging in particular trade, financial activities, or other dealings with sanctioned parties unless they have permission from OFAC or are specifically allowed by law.[4] Since each sanctions program is based on different foreign policy and national security goals, prohibitions can vary from one program to another.[5]

Why Are Sanctions Used?

Sanctions are used instead of military force to change the behavior of individuals or governments. The goal is to alter their behavior without resorting to violence.

Specific reasons sanctions are imposed include:

- address human rights violations
- support democracy
- stop extremist groups by cutting off key resources needed to continue their activities
- protect national security interests
- protect international law
- preserve peace
- coerce a regime into changing its behavior or isolate the regime as a way of sending a broader political message internationally

- prevent conflicts and strengthen international security

What Countries Use Them?

Many countries have their own sanctions laws, likely including your own. Some jurisdictions include the US, UK, Canada, Japan, and Australia. Even the European Union, which is comprised of many countries, has its own sanctions regime. Countries that are part of the EU must follow the sanctions set by the EU,[6] but they can also add more prohibitions of their own.

If your company does business in multiple countries, you might need to follow sanctions regulations from several countries.

What Governmental Agency Is Responsible for Them?

The Office of Foreign Assets Control (OFAC), part of the US Department of the Treasury, oversees most US sanctions programs. OFAC enforces US sanctions laws civilly, while the US Department of Justice handles criminal violations.

Some trade sanctions are managed by different agencies like the Department of State (DoS) and the Bureau of Industry and Security (BIS) of the Department of Commerce. These export control restrictions work alongside OFAC sanctions and will be discussed in more detail later in this guide.

How Are Sanctions Programs Created?

Most sanctions programs are established and administered through Executive Orders, laws, and regulations.

US sanctions programs are based on laws passed by Congress. These laws give the President the emergency power to limit or prohibit international financial transactions, imports and exports, or entry into the US.[7] One such law is the Trading with the Enemy Act (TWEA). You don't need to know all the details of these laws to maintain an effective sanctions program, but it is important to understand they are what allow sanctions programs to exist.

Congress can also issue new sanctions directly via regulations, such as the Countering America's Adversaries Through Sanctions Act (CAATSA), which provides additional sanctions on Russia, Ukraine, Iran, and North Korea.

When the President wants to impose new sanctions (under the authority of one of the previously mentioned laws), he will issue an Executive Order. The Executive Order explains why sanctions are needed, the laws under which the Executive Order is created (like TWEA), and who can be sanctioned under the program.

As time passes, more Executive Orders might get added to a program, expanding the scope of activity and parties that can be sanctioned. For example, the Russian Harmful Foreign Activities program has grown to include six Executive Orders. These orders prohibit additional activities like importing certain products from Russia into the US or investing in certain parts of the Russian economy. [8]

OFAC will incorporate the sanctions laws and Executive Orders into its own regulations for a program, which are issued in the Code of Federal Regulations (CFR). The CFR is where all rules implemented by the Federal government are published. For example, the Lebanese Program is codified at 31 CFR Part 549 Lebanon Sanction Regulations.[9]

Some programs operate only via Executive Order and do not have regulations published. For example, the Afghanistan program does not have OFAC-related regulations issued for it.[10]

It is essential to familiarize yourself with the CFR regulations for each OFAC program to understand what activity is allowed and what is not under the program. However, not all the information you need to comply with the program will be in the CFR regulations. Later, I'll discuss other helpful resources, such as guidance, general licenses, and frequently asked questions (FAQs), that are specific to a program but won't be found in the CFR.

Sanctions Programs

OFAC administers sanctions programs that consist of all the laws, Executive Orders, OFAC regulations, guidance, licenses, and FAQs related to restrictions against a specific country or activity. Some programs target activities in certain countries, such as Cuba, while some target specific activities globally, such as narcotics trafficking and weapons proliferation.

A country-based program does not mean that only people in that country are sanctioned. Parties anywhere in the world can be sanctioned under any program, including those in the US as well as those in your country. For example, the Russian Harmful Foreign Activities Program imposes sanctions against individuals and entities anywhere in the world involved in specified harmful foreign activities of the Russian Federation.[11]

Also, programs may not exist indefinitely. For example, Sudan used to have a trade embargo, but it was discontinued several years ago, and Sudan is currently subject to only minimal sanctions.

The best place to find all of these documents is under the specific program's page on the OFAC website, the link for which is provided under References.

2
Types of Sanctions

The term "sanctions" covers a wide range of actions the United States can take against a country, government, person, group, or industry, depending on what activity the US wants to stop. Generally, sanctions fall into three main categories: comprehensive, list-based, and sectoral or trade.[12] Let's take a closer look at each one.

Comprehensive

Comprehensive sanctions, or trade embargoes, apply to a whole country. They restrict almost all commercial and financial activities involving the sanctioned country, including its government, individuals, businesses, and anyone acting on behalf of that country.[13]

Countries like Cuba, Iran, Syria, North Korea, and specific areas of Ukraine under Russian control, such as Crimea, face comprehensive sanctions from the US. However, current sanctions against Russia are nearly as comprehensive.

Even with comprehensive sanctions, some business activities are still allowed in these countries. We'll explore this further in a later chapter.

List-Based

OFAC uses different types of watchlists to enforce sanctions, with sanctioned parties placed on either the Specially Designated Nationals (SDN) list, which carries full blocking prohibitions, or a Non-SDN list, which has more targeted restrictions. Each list serves a different purpose, so if you find a customer is sanctioned, you must know which list they're on and what specific restrictions apply. A party can also appear on more than one watchlist. Let's dive into these lists in more detail.

The Specially Designated Nationals (SDN) List

When a party is sanctioned under an OFAC blocking program, they are added to the "Specially Designated Nationals" (SDN) list. A wide range of parties can end up on the SDN list, including individuals, companies, groups, ships, aircraft, and even cryptocurrency wallets.

Parties on the SDN list will face penalties like asset freezes, travel restrictions, import/export bans, and financial prohibitions.[14] US persons and businesses are not allowed to conduct any transactions with SDNs. These measures are intended to deprive the SDN of economic resources that could support the activities the US wants to prevent. Later chapters will provide guidance on steps to take if a customer appears on the SDN list.

One example of a blocking program is the Global Magnitsky Sanctions Regulations.[15] The "Prohibited Transactions" section of these regulations states that "all property and interests in property... are blocked," which means you must stop all business with any party listed under this program.[16]

Non-SDN Lists

Parties on Non-SDN lists are not SDNs and are not subject to full blocking prohibitions like those on the SDN list. Instead, they are subject to specific penalties, including export controls, import bans, financial transaction restrictions, and sectoral sanctions (i.e., restrictions on particular industries).

There are several non-SDN lists, each with different purposes, including:[17]

Sectoral Sanctions Identifications (SSI) List

This list targets specific sectors of the economy and the parties operating within them. It is used primarily in the Ukraine-/Russia-related Sanctions program.[18] Restrictions are set through official orders known as "Directives," which outline the prohibited activities.

A Directive is a determination issued by the President to ban certain activities under an Executive Order. There might be limits on debt or equity, import/export controls, or restrictions on specific sectors like energy, defense, or finance. For example, if an entity is sanctioned under Directive 1, US persons are not allowed to engage in transactions involving new debt with a maturity longer than fourteen days or new equity of this entity.[19]

Even though the SSI restricts certain activities by designated parties, other dealings with these entities are still allowed, and their assets aren't frozen.

Non-SDN Menu-Based Sanctions List (NS-MBS List)

Parties on this list are not SDNs and are not subject to full blocking sanctions like those on the SDN list. Each party on the list can have different prohibitions. Their assets aren't blocked, but they face trade or financial restrictions, like restrictions on receiving certain goods or services.[20]

For example, under the Counter Narcotics Trafficking Sanctions program, parties sanctioned under Executive Order 14059 may be restricted from receiving loans or credit, among other prohibitions.[21]

Non-SDN Chinese Military-Industrial Complex Companies List (NS-CMIC List)

These are Chinese companies that OFAC has determined have Chinese military ties. Again, they are not subject to full blocking sanctions. Instead, OFAC prohibits investment in these companies (i.e., purchasing their debt or equity, such as stocks, bonds, or the mutual funds that invest in them).

Sectoral or Trade Sanctions

Sectoral or trade sanctions can be challenging to understand because they prohibit specific activities with designated entities in certain industries while allowing other activities to continue. These sanctions may also ban certain goods from being imported from or exported to a sanctioned country. The purpose is to weaken the country economically by targeting its most significant industries, thereby pushing it to end its unwanted behavior.

By definition, comprehensively sanctioned countries have trade sanctions. Sectoral sanctions, as discussed in the prior section, target certain sectors of the economy and specific parties operating in them. On the other hand, trade sanctions restrict imports and exports of goods and services to and from a sanctioned country. Let's discuss these types of trade sanctions and how they are used, using Russia as an example.

Targeting Industries

In Russia, sectoral sanctions impact major industries, such as energy, finance, minerals, and mining. Entities in these sectors may face either blocking sanctions or specific restrictions under non-SDN sanctions.

For example, on September 15, 2022, OFAC authorized sanctions on individuals and entities operating in the quantum computing sector of Russia.[22]

Targeting Services

US persons are banned from providing certain services to parties in Russia, including quantum computing, architecture, engineering, accounting, trust and corporate formation, and management consulting.[23] US parties that do business in these sectors in Russia can be sanctioned. These prohibitions are established via Determinations, which are orders issued once it has been determined that a specific activity is prohibited under a previously issued Executive Order (E.O.).

For example, on September 15, 2022, OFAC issued a Determination under E.O. 14071 that USK persons cannot provide quantum computing services to anyone in Russia.[24] This service prohibition works in tandem with the related sectoral sanction targeting the industry to basically shut off any quantum computing-related activities in Russia.

However, the restrictions do not prohibit US persons from providing other services not covered by these sanctions.[25]

Some countries, like the UK and the EU, may have different service prohibitions.

Targeting Imports/Exports

Trade sanctions can ban the import of certain Russian goods into the US, such as fish and seafood, alcohol, and diamonds;[26] oil and petroleum products;[27] and Russian-origin aluminum, copper, and nickel,[28] among other items.

OFAC, along with the Bureau of Industry and Security (BIS) and the Department of State (DoS), has also restricted the export of many US-origin items to Russia, including electronics, mechanical components, technical parts, manufacturing equipment, machine tools, and items that could be used in Russia's military systems.[29]

Foreign companies doing business in countries facing OFAC import/export restrictions must ensure that their products are not US-origin or do not contain US-origin parts, as we'll discuss further in a later chapter.

Again, sectoral and trade sanctions do not ban US persons from all transactions with targeted companies—only those involving restricted activities or goods.

Sanctioned Parties Not on Any List

The most challenging part of complying with US sanctions is when parties are considered sanctioned despite not appearing on any SDN or Non-SDN watchlist. This can occur in a couple of ways.

First, some OFAC sanctions block categories of persons even if they are not listed on a watchlist.[30] For example, for the Venezuelan sanctions program, Executive Order 13884 blocks any person who meets the definition of the "Government of Venezuela."[31] Also, OFAC's Cuba sanctions prohibit most transactions with Cuban nationals.[32]

The second way is commonly referred to as the "50 Percent Rule."[33] This rule kicks in when a company is majority-owned (50 percent or more) by one or more sanctioned parties. This includes both direct and indirect ownership. These entities are still considered sanctioned even if they aren't listed on a watchlist.

No official government list of companies owned by sanctioned parties exists, but some private companies, like Dow Jones, create and maintain such lists.

Let's look at an example of how this works. Goode Company has three owners: Bad Co., which is on the SDN list, owns 30 percent of the company; Worst Inc., which is also on the SDN list, owns 25 percent of the company; Best LLC, which is not on the SDN list, owns the remaining 45 percent. Because two of the owners of Goode Company are SDNs, and together they own 55 percent of the company (a majority), Goode Company is also considered an SDN, even though they are not on the SDN list.

Note that Best LLC is not sanctioned, despite being an owner of Goode Company and a partner with Bad Co. and Worst Inc. Just because a branch or subsidiary is sanctioned does not automatically make a parent company sanctioned.

The example above dealt with direct ownership. This gets more complicated when indirect ownership is involved.

Let's use the Goode Company example again.

Goode Company has three owners: Bad Co. owns 30 percent, Worst Inc. owns 25 percent, and Best LLC owns 45 percent. None of these three entities is on an SDN list. However, Bad Co. and Worst Inc. are both 50 percent owned by Sanctioned Person A, so both are deemed sanctioned. Therefore, with 55 percent ownership by sanctioned parties, Goode Company is also considered sanctioned due to its majority indirect ownership by Sanctioned Person A.

When parties are sanctioned, they frequently divest part of their ownership in entities where they are the majority owners so that the entities are not deemed sanctioned. For example, to avoid being blocked by Russian sanctions, some majority owners of Russian companies, like Rusal, divested part or all of their ownership to fall just below the 50 percent mark. [34]

The US's 50 Percent Rule functions differently from the UK's and the EU's 50 Percent Rule, which will be discussed in a later chapter.

3
Who Has To Comply with US Economic Sanctions?

OFAC's definition of who has to comply with US sanctions is broad and can include persons or entities not located or operating within the US.

You are required to comply with US sanctions if one of the following conditions exists:
- You are covered under the definition of a US Person.
- You are conducting a transaction with a US nexus.
- You are conducting an activity covered by OFAC's secondary sanctions.

Who Is a Covered US Person?

You are a US Person and are covered by US sanctions in the following situations:

- US citizens anywhere in the world
- US-incorporated businesses, including their foreign branches
- people in the US for any reason, even if they are citizens of another country
- any party using the US financial system, US dollars, or US goods[35]

This means a foreign bank without US branches must also follow OFAC rules if it uses US dollars or the US financial system for a transaction.

Foreign Subsidiaries of US Entities

If you work for a foreign company with a US parent company, it's essential to understand whether your company operates as a branch or a subsidiary of the US parent. If it is a branch, it must always follow OFAC rules. However, subsidiaries generally do not fall under the definition of a US person, as OFAC defines a US person as a business incorporated in the United States and its foreign branches. However, the Iran, Cuba, and North Korea sanctions programs have expanded the meaning of a US person to include foreign subsidiaries.

- Cuba – The Cuban regulation defines "persons subject to the jurisdiction of the United States,"[36] which, in short, includes any

entity, wherever organized or doing business, owned or controlled by a US person. This would include foreign subsidiaries.
- Iran – Iranian regulations prohibit "an entity owned or controlled by a US person, set up outside the US," from dealing with Iran's government or citizens if that activity would be prohibited when conducted by a US person.[37] Again, this definition includes foreign subsidiaries.
- North Korea – North Korean regulations prohibit "a person owned or controlled by a US financial institution and established or maintained outside the United States" from conducting transactions with the Government of North Korea or a party sanctioned under North Korean regulations.[38] This definition would include foreign subsidiaries of US financial institutions.

So, if your foreign company is a subsidiary of a US company and you sometimes do business in Cuba, Iran, or North Korea, you might get a warning from your sanctions compliance team not to conduct that business. If you ignore the warning, your company could face penalties from OFAC.

US-Nexus Transactions

There are other times when foreign companies might need to follow US sanctions. This happens when a transaction has a connection, or nexus, to the United States. Here are some examples of transactions a foreign company can conduct with a US nexus (this is not a complete list of possibilities):

- conducting transactions through a US-based branch or subsidiary
- providing insurance that covers activity in the US
- a foreign subsidiary of a US company providing insurance coverage to a customer with property in Iran
- conducting a transaction where a US person is involved in any way
- purchasing, transporting, or insuring goods that are of US origin or contain US-origin parts anywhere in the world
- doing business through a US financial institution or a foreign branch of a US financial institution
- making or receiving a payment using US dollars

Correspondent banking is another way foreign companies and banks can unknowingly connect their transactions to the US, leading to sanctions violations. In correspondent banking, a US financial institution acts as a middleman for a foreign bank, allowing it to access the US banking system through a single account. All the transactions from the foreign bank's customers go through this one account.

For example, Swedbank Latvia, a subsidiary of a foreign bank, was fined by OFAC for hundreds of transactions that violated sanctions on Crimea. A customer used Swedbank Latvia's online banking platform from a sanctioned jurisdiction to send payments to others also located in a sanctioned jurisdiction through Swedbank's US correspondent banks.[39]

Another way to have a US nexus is through omnibus accounts. Omnibus accounts are held with brokers and function like correspondent accounts, where one account combines all of a customer's assets and trades managed by a custodian. If your company uses omnibus accounts or trades through an omnibus account with a broker who is considered a US person, this creates a US nexus, which can lead to an OFAC violation.

In several instances, OFAC has fined foreign companies for not following OFAC rules while using the US financial system. For example, Toll Holdings, based in Australia, was fined by OFAC for routing payments through US financial institutions for shipments to or through comprehensively sanctioned countries or involving SDNs.[40]

Secondary Sanctions

Some US sanctions go beyond US borders (i.e., have "extraterritorial reach"). These are secondary sanctions.

Secondary sanctions are penalties imposed by one country on individuals, entities, or governments in another country for engaging in activities that violate the first country's sanctions or policies.[41] This means OFAC can require foreign parties not considered US persons to follow its rules or risk getting sanctioned themselves. Usually, the punishment involved being shut out of the US financial system. Iran, North Korea, and Russia are examples of programs with secondary sanctions.

Here are a couple of examples of how this has worked recently:

- In 2018, the US left the Joint Comprehensive Plan of Action (JCPOA) agreement, which loosened sanctions on Iran in exchange for restrictions on Iran's nuclear program. After leaving the JCPOA, the US reinstated sanctions on Iran, including secondary sanctions for non-US parties trading with Iran in areas like energy, precious metals, finance, and software.[42]
- In late 2023, the US issued a new Executive Order 14114 concerning Russia.[43] It required foreign financial institutions (FFIs) to follow certain US sanctions against Russia. Specifically, FFIs can't conduct transactions for a sanctioned party in key sectors of the Russian economy, including technology, defense, aerospace, and manufacturing. Nor can they conduct any transaction or provide any service or good to Russia's military. OFAC defines foreign financial institutions as banks, insurance companies, and broker-dealers, among other entities. So, a foreign subsidiary of a US-based financial institution, not otherwise subject to OFAC's Russian-related sanctions, would have to follow these restrictions as an FFI.

Foreign companies must know what activity violates OFAC's secondary sanctions to avoid being shut out of the US financial system. With secondary sanctions, a foreign entity's transactions do not have to have a US nexus to be considered a violation by OFAC. It just has to violate the activity under which OFAC has implemented prohibitions.

For example, in May 2021, several Russian parties involved in constructing the Nord Stream 2 pipeline to Germany were sanctioned, none of whom were US persons.

In another instance, the US imposed secondary sanctions on Syrian businessmen for entering into otherwise legal contracts with the Syrian government without a US nexus. The US claimed they were "knowingly providing significant financial, material, or technological support to, or knowingly engaging in a significant transaction with, the Government of Syria."[44]

So, your foreign company will likely need to comply with US sanctions regulations at some point to avoid US penalties, including sanctions.

4
Other Nuances about OFAC Sanctions

You can see by now that OFAC sanctions are not straightforward and are open to interpretation. Here are a few key things to know about sanctions that aren't so obvious in the regulations but are critical to ensuring sanctions compliance.

US Territory

US territory includes more than fifty states and the District of Columbia. It is broadly defined as "the United States, its territories and possessions, and all areas under the jurisdiction or authority."[45] For example, American Samoa and Guam are US territories, so they are not considered foreign countries when it comes to OFAC sanctions. "Areas under jurisdiction" include places under US control in foreign countries, like military bases and embassies. So, business in those areas isn't seen as happening on foreign soil. For instance, Guantanamo Bay in Cuba isn't covered by Cuban sanctions because it is technically under US jurisdiction, not Cuba's. If you do business in these areas, you should be aware that OFAC regulations apply there.

Indirect

OFAC prohibits both direct and indirect provision of prohibited goods or services. "Direct" is self-explanatory, but what is "indirect?"

If a company sells goods or services to someone acting on behalf of a sanctioned party or country, even without knowing it, they are indirectly doing business with that sanctioned party. For example, if a firm sells US-made computer parts to a wholesaler in India, who then sells the parts to customers in Russia or Cuba—where the firm is not allowed to sell directly—the firm is indirectly supplying prohibited goods.

An example is Alfa Laval Middle East, which OFAC fined for causing its US affiliate to indirectly export goods from the US to Iran. They did this by falsely listing a Dubai-based company as the end-user on their export paperwork.[46]

Facilitation

"Facilitation" means helping others break sanctions rules. It could be offering financial help, organizing support, or providing aid that lets sanctioned people, groups, or countries avoid sanctions.[47] A US person cannot facilitate a transaction that, if they had conducted it themselves, would violate OFAC sanctions.

Facilitation could be as simple as referring prohibited business to another company not covered by the OFAC regulation. Our organization was concerned that even referring business to our UK subsidiary when our domestic companies couldn't write those policies might be considered facilitation.

OFAC doesn't allow facilitation, and breaking this rule can have severe legal consequences, as it weakens sanctions and supports illegal actions. For example, AL Tank in the US violated Iranian sanctions by referring an Iranian business opportunity to their Middle East affiliate, thereby facilitating a transaction that would have been prohibited if performed by the US entity.[48]

Sanctions Evasion

Sanctions evasion happens when people try to hide or structure transactions to get around sanctions. Common tactics include using straw buyers, creating fake companies, transferring assets to non-sanctioned relatives, trading through third countries, hiding the true origin of goods, or setting up new companies in countries not under sanctions.

For instance, say someone's sanctioned under the Lebanon sanctions program, and a company wants to sell them an appliance. The SDN uses a third party to buy it for them. If the selling company knows or should have known through due diligence that a transaction will ultimately benefit a sanctioned person, they could get into big trouble with OFAC.

In another example, if a foreign entity wants to do business with a sanctioned party, it might falsify or omit information regarding the sanctioned party on wire transfers when using a US bank. This is considered sanctions evasion by OFAC.

Non-US persons are also prohibited from causing US persons to knowingly or unknowingly violate US sanctions by engaging in conduct that evades US sanctions, even if they themselves are not directly breaking the law.[49]

One example is when OFAC fined CSE TransTel, a company based in Singapore, for causing sanctions violations. TransTel did business with Iran and helped a non-US financial institution violate sanctions by purposely concealing the origin or destination of US dollar payments destined for Iranian companies.[50]

Globality of Sanctioned Parties

People and entities worldwide can be listed as SDNs under any OFAC program. For example, a program covering Russia does not mean only Russian entities are sanctioned under it. Parties in India, China, and even Europe can be sanctioned under this program.

Additionally, parties in countries without formal sanctions programs, including the US, can be sanctioned under any program, such as those sanctioned under the narcotics trafficking program.

If you handle a transaction with a US nexus and aren't checking the names of all parties, wherever located, against OFAC watchlists, you have a gap in your compliance process. This gap could result in an OFAC violation. We had a situation where a foreign broker of one of our policies only scanned the names of policyholders located in sanctioned countries. When we checked the policyholder's name, we discovered they were sanctioned based on Iranian ownership despite not being located in a sanctioned country.

Globality of Insurance

If you work for a foreign insurance company that offers global (i.e., worldwide) policies, you might have a US nexus. For example, if your company provides life insurance, that policy will likely cover the policyholder anywhere in the world, including the US. Similarly, if you offer global travel insurance, it would also cover travel to the US.

OFAC allows global coverage for life, health, and travel insurance, even in sanctioned areas, as long as the policy covers the rest of the world (meaning it cannot be specific to just one country).

However, there are some restrictions. If you have a policy with a US nexus (for instance, if your parent company is based in the US), and the customer goes to Iran and dies, you may be able to pay the death benefit to the beneficiary. However, you might not be allowed to pay Iranian companies for returning the body or for government documents related to the death without permission from OFAC via a specific license.

United Nations (UN) Requirements

As a United Nations member, the US also requires its citizens and businesses to follow UN sanctions. Your country may already comply with UN sanctions, but if it doesn't, review these rules (link in References). Generally, if you follow OFAC regulations, you're likely also meeting UN sanctions requirements. When screening for OFAC compliance, you should also check the UN's sanctions watchlists.

Multiple Jurisdictions May Be Involved

If your company does business globally, you will need to follow sanctions regimes in every country where you do business, which can result in several jurisdictions for one transaction.

An example of how this works:

You are a company located in the UK with a Swedish subsidiary that wants to sell computer parts to a Russian entity. The computer parts are US-origin, although currently located with a wholesaler in China.

How many jurisdictions do you have to comply with sanctions in?

- The parent company is in the UK, so there is a UK nexus.
- The subsidiary is in Sweden, so there is a Swedish and EU nexus since Sweden is part of the EU.
- The goods are of US origin, so there is a US nexus.
- The goods are in China, so there is a Chinese nexus.
- The customer is in Russia, a high-risk jurisdiction. The policy is subject to US, UK, and EU sanctions programs over Russia, each with subtle differences regarding Russian imports.

Therefore, for one transaction, you may have to comply with US, UK, and EU sanctions, or more, simultaneously!

US Sanctions Can Differ from Other Jurisdictions

However, be aware that sanctions regimes differ from country to country, so don't fall into the trap of thinking that if a transaction is legal to conduct in one country, it is okay in another.

Here are some examples of how sanctions rules differ by jurisdiction, using a comparison of US sanctions versus EU and UK sanctions:

- The US is the only major economy that has a sanctions program against Cuba.
- The EU and the UK have "blocking statutes,"[51] which prevent anyone under EU or UK jurisdiction from following regulations that conflict with their own. As such, they don't allow parties to comply with OFAC sanctions (such as for Iran and Cuba) when they conflict with the EU's and UK's sanctions programs. This will be discussed in detail in a later chapter.
- The EU and the UK have sanctions programs against some countries that the US does not, such as Tunisia and Guinea-Bissau. Therefore, it's important to ensure you comply with the sanctions for any jurisdiction involved in the transaction, even if it wouldn't violate OFAC rules.
- The EU's and the UK's lists of designated parties may differ from OFAC's watchlists and each other's. You should also check the watchlists for every jurisdiction in which you do business.
- The EU and the UK may have sanctions programs targeting the same countries as the US, but their restrictions often differ. For example, the UK and the EU have sanctions programs against Venezuela. However, unlike the US, the EU does not ban transactions with the Venezuelan government or Petróleos de Venezuela (PdVSA), the country's largest energy producer. Similarly, while the US has a complete trade embargo against Iran, the UK and the EU have less restrictive sanctions. Their rules mainly focus on exports of goods or technology that could be used in weapons or military applications.
- The 50 Percent Rule applies to ownership *and control* in the EU and the UK, while in the US, it applies only to ownership. When conducting business in the EU or the UK with SDNs who control the

company (including minority owners, executives, or board members), be cautious, as they may be viewed as holding majority control. This can be challenging to determine in practice, so consulting legal counsel is recommended if you encounter this situation. It's also important to note that the UK's 50 percent threshold starts at 50.01 percent ownership, or "more than 50 percent," while the US and EU set it at 50.00 percent or more. This distinction can be significant, as sanctioned parties sometimes reduce their ownership to just below the threshold. For example, if a sanctioned party owns exactly 50.00 percent of a company, that company would be sanctioned under OFAC but not in the UK. Additionally, the UK does not combine ownership stakes among sanctioned parties to determine if an entity meets the 50 Percent Rule unless the rights are under a joint arrangement or one party controls another's rights.

Therefore, don't assume that sanctions restrictions in your country mirror the US's restrictions or vice versa.

5
Trade Sanctions

Foreign companies importing or exporting US-origin goods must consider requirements from two additional agencies beyond OFAC: the Bureau of Industry and Security (BIS) and the Department of State (DoS). While OFAC enforces import and export restrictions on certain countries and individuals, BIS and the DoS focus on licensing specific items, mainly dual-use, military, and defense products. They also maintain lists of restricted parties who cannot sell or receive these goods.

Although BIS and DoS primarily require licenses for sensitive items, their controls are intended to prevent these goods from aiding foreign military and defense sectors. OFAC's trade sanctions, in contrast, cover a broader range of industries, prohibiting many kinds of import/export transactions with specific countries and individuals, some of which overlap with the BIS and DoS oversight. Businesses often need to comply with all three agencies.

For foreign companies dealing with countries under OFAC's import/export sanctions, it's essential to ensure that products don't contain US-origin parts or weren't made in the US, as this could lead to violations of both OFAC sanctions and BIS and DoS import/export rules.

What Is a US-Origin Good?

A good is considered US origin if it is "all or virtually all" made in the United States. The origin is based on where the product was manufactured, not where it's shipped from. Items located in or passing through the US are also of US origin. Additionally, goods made outside the US that contain at least 25 percent US-origin content (10 percent for embargoed countries) or are directly made using US technology or software are also considered US origin.[52] Therefore, foreign-produced items can still be US-origin if they contain US-origin parts, technology, or software.

Other US Government Agencies That Enforce Trade Sanctions

Bureau of Industry and Security (BIS)

The US Department of Commerce's Bureau of Industry and Security (BIS) administers and enforces export controls on dual-use and military items through the Export Administration Regulations (EAR). The EAR applies to the item anywhere in the world and foreign parties dealing with it. This includes situations where the item is re-exported between foreign countries or transferred within a foreign country.

For example, an exporter cannot bypass the US embargo against Iran by shipping an item to a distributor in the United Arab Emirates.[53]

Both BIS and OFAC can impose fines on foreign companies for violating the EAR if the transaction also violates an economic sanction. For example, Alcon Laboratory in Switzerland was fined by both OFAC and BIS after selling and exporting unlicensed medical end-use surgical and pharmaceutical products from the United States to distributors in Iran and Sudan without OFAC authorization.[54]

Department of State (DoS)

The Department of State has several divisions that oversee the export of defense-related items and services under the Arms Export Control Act (AECA), the International Traffic in Arms Regulations (ITAR), and the United States Munitions List (USML). These include the Directorate of Defense Trade Controls (DDTC) and the Bureau of International Security and Non-Proliferation (ISN).

The DDTC controls commercial exports of defense articles and services. They enforce the AECA and the ITAR and can impose penalties for violations. If a company or person violates the AECA, they can be debarred, meaning they are banned from exporting defense goods and services. There are two types of debarment: statutory, which happens after a criminal conviction, and administrative, which results from a DDTC enforcement action. Debarred parties can apply for reinstatement of their export privileges after a set period.[55]

The ISN works to prevent the spread of weapons of mass destruction (WMDs), such as nuclear, chemical, and biological weapons.[56] It focuses on preventing the unauthorized trade of materials that could be used to make WMDs.

You could violate OFAC as well as BIS or DoS trade sanctions if you sell US-origin goods that require a license to sanctioned parties or sanctioned countries. The types of goods that need an export license are not always obvious. We once had a customer on the BIS list for exporting straitjackets without a license. The DoS listed another customer for sending US technology diagrams to their Chinese subsidiary for work. Although OFAC sanctioned neither customer, we still had to make sure we were not insuring any illegal exports from these companies to avoid violating BIS or DoS restrictions.

If you buy, sell, or insure US-origin goods, both BIS and DoS have their own watchlists that you should check when screening for sanctions, in addition to the OFAC watchlists. The DoS has two watchlists: the DDTC debarred list and the ISN non-proliferation sanctions list. The BIS maintains four watchlists: two lists of users who can't receive licensable goods, one list of foreign parties subject to more restrictive licensing requirements to export goods, and one list of persons denied export privileges.

One particular advisory every foreign entity should review is the Department of Commerce, Department of the Treasury, and Department of Justice "Tri-Seal Compliance Note: Obligations of foreign-based persons to comply with US sanctions and export control laws" (link provided under Resources), which is explicitly directed at foreign companies involved in global trade.

6
How Economic Sanctions Affect Your Company

Economic sanctions impact your entire organization—every employee, every department, and every business line—especially in global enterprises. So, your company is likely affected.

While sanctions compliance professionals are directly involved, the responsibility doesn't stop there. Employees handling tasks with a sanctions nexus must also understand and adhere to sanctions requirements. When their work involves transactions connected to the US, their roles become even more complex, requiring a basic understanding of OFAC sanctions.

This list isn't exhaustive, but it highlights key roles that may have a sanctions nexus that will need sanctions procedures and training within your organization:

- payment processors (such as a payment for goods or services, claim, refund, or vendor payment)
- originate a payment on an account
- open new accounts
- underwrite policies or loans
- conduct customer due diligence
- import or export goods
- conduct marine shipments
- contract with vendors or other business partners
- sell products or services
- hire staff
- claims adjustors
- product development
- legal/compliance
- customer service

Let's look at a few examples of how the jobs listed above can encounter sanctions issues:

- Accounts Receivable (AR): AR invoices customers and receives payments. If AR invoices Joe Designee in the US, this creates a US nexus. In addition to checking Joe Designee's name against local sanctions lists, AR must also check OFAC watchlists. AR staff may need to scan names manually before invoicing and prior to posting payments unless an automated system handles this. At a minimum, AR staff should understand that OFAC rules apply in these cases so they can respond appropriately if compliance needs extra information or funds need to be blocked.

- Sales: Sales teams who handle product sales need to understand sanctions regulations to avoid selling to sanctioned parties or shipping restricted goods to sanctioned countries, especially US-origin products. They should be cautious to avoid any actions leading to illegal transaction structuring, sanctions evasion, facilitating illicit transactions, or indirect sales to sanctioned parties.
- Shipping: The shipping department must be aware of sanctions and know how to identify any issues involving OFAC, such as shipments containing US-origin goods or involving US entities (e.g., a US-based shipping company). They should gather necessary shipment details and know when to flag shipments for sanctions review. For instance, if a US-origin product is being shipped to Russia, they should ensure it's reviewed to confirm it's not a prohibited item or going to a sanctioned party.
- Claims Adjusting: Claims adjusters review claims and approve payments. Before any payment is issued, all payees must be checked against sanctions lists. For international payments, they need to confirm the country isn't comprehensively sanctioned and that the payment isn't going to a sanctioned bank. Adjusters must understand OFAC sanctions, as there are many ways a claim can have an OFAC nexus through the goods involved, involved parties (like vendors), or connections to the US financial system. A claim with a US nexus could cause compliance issues if an adjuster doesn't identify it and refer it for a sanctions review.
- Underwriting: Underwriters evaluate insurance applications and determine coverage. Before issuing a policy, all included parties—such as the primary insured, additional insureds, contractors, and counterparties—should be screened against sanctions watchlists. Underwriters should also be able to identify other sanctions risks, like

coverage in sanctioned countries and whether an OFAC nexus in a new policy may affect issuance, and know to refer those issues to sanctions compliance for review.

If you think about it, there are few jobs within a company without a sanctions nexus, and likely few jobs in a global company that won't occasionally encounter a US connection in a transaction they are conducting. So, it's vital that all employees are trained in basic OFAC sanctions and that your organization has procedures for these employees to follow.

7
How Do I Comply with OFAC Sanctions?

OFAC prohibits all parties subject to US sanctions from doing business with sanctioned parties. How you comply is up to you.

Start by setting up a basic sanctions compliance program that outlines how you will comply with regulations. Foreign companies should review OFAC's guidance on sanctions program compliance (link in References). If you already have a program, compare it to OFAC's recommendations to identify necessary improvements.

Below is a basic outline of what you might want to include in your sanctions compliance program. This outline is based on real-life experience, industry best practices, and OFAC guidance. [57]

Establish a Sanctions Program

A sanctions compliance program (SCP) is comprised of the policies, procedures, and controls that help a company follow sanctions regulations.

At a minimum, a company should have a sanctions compliance program that encompasses:

- a Sanctions Compliance Officer (SCO) or other responsible party
- an economic sanctions policy
- written procedures
- a risk assessment
- customer and vendor due diligence
- training
- internal controls
- contract language
- environmental scanning
- auditing and testing

Let's discuss these key sections of an SCP in more detail.

Responsible Party

Your program will identify who in the company is responsible for overseeing sanctions compliance. This should be someone who manages all aspects of the program, directly supervises the sanctions compliance team, and indirectly oversees any additional staff performing sanctions-related duties. This can be a sanctions compliance officer (SCO) or the head of your sanctions compliance team. Alternatively, it could be someone with sufficient authority within the organization, such as the chief compliance officer (CCO) or the chief legal officer (CLO).

The SCO should have enough independence and authority to act within the company. Ideally, this should be someone at the management level or higher. The person should be allowed to take the necessary actions to address any issues with the sanctions program. They should have direct access to senior management without going through several other management layers. Periodic meetings with senior management should occur to provide updates on the status of the sanctions program.

Some responsibilities of the sanctions compliance officer include:
- maintaining and updating the economic sanctions policy
- developing procedures
- conducting the risk assessment
- overseeing staff who perform sanctions-related procedures
- administering sanctions training
- working with other teams within the company to implement sanctions controls
- updating senior management on sanctions issues and projects
- acting as a liaison with external legal counsel
- filing required reports with OFAC

Sanctions Policy

The cornerstone of the SCP is an economic sanctions policy. The policy will outline your company's commitment to sanctions compliance and briefly describe the procedures and controls for compliance.

Key best practices when drafting or updating your sanctions policy:
- It should be risk-based and tailored to your company's specific risks.
- It should be written in plain, easy-to-read language since everyone in the company must be familiar with it.
- If employees are located in foreign countries, it should be translated into their native language.

- It should be reviewed and updated annually or whenever significant updates are made to sanctions regulations or your program.
- It should be stored in an area (such as an online shared site) where all staff can review it.

Here are some sections to include:

- senior management's commitment to fostering a culture of compliance
- pertinent definitions for key terms such as sanctions, sanctioned parties, prohibited transactions, etc.
- potential penalties to the company and the individual for non-compliance
- who the policy applies to in the company, and whether third parties such as vendors and business partners must comply with your policy
- sanctions laws applicable to your company, both domestic and foreign
- high-level description of internal controls
- the person responsible for the program and their duties
- how a risk assessment will be conducted
- who will receive sanctions training
- testing and auditing of the program
- methods to report potential violations

Store this policy in an area (such as an online shared site) where all staff can review it.

Written Procedures

Any procedures supporting sanctions-related processes should be in writing. This shows OFAC, auditors, and internal parties like the CCO that procedures are in place and how they work, and it serves as a valuable training tool for new staff.

Here are some procedures you might consider for your company for OFAC compliance:

- how to review and clear alerts from a scanning application
- how and when to manually scan business
- when other departments should refer business to the sanctions compliance team or SCO for review

- what steps to take if a customer is sanctioned
- how to escalate sanctions issues (such as a potential violation)
- how to conduct a risk assessment
- how and when should OFAC be contacted to file blocked assets and rejected transaction reports, apply for specific licenses, file a voluntary self-disclosure, etc.

Procedures should be reviewed and updated at least annually or when there is a significant update to a process.

Risk Assessment

A risk assessment is a method for identifying, analyzing, and addressing a company's exposure to sanctions-related risks. It helps pinpoint any weaknesses in the compliance program and lays out a plan to fix them. Your sanctions compliance program should be based on risk. Include US sanctions risks in your risk assessment, along with specific risks for other jurisdictions in which you regularly do business. A risk assessment should be updated at least annually.

The Plain-English Guide to Economic Sanctions Risk Assessments and its related workbook can assist you in developing your risk assessment with easy-to-use worksheets that cover every step in the process.

Customer and Vendor Due Diligence

A company should do two types of checks to spot possible sanctions problems before moving forward with business: one for its customers and another for its third-party business partners.

Due diligence means getting to know your customers and vendors to understand their risks. This includes the following procedures:
- checking customer and vendor names against sanctions watchlists
- finding out who owns and runs the business (beneficial ownership)
- scanning beneficial owners' names against sanctions watchlists
- looking for any sanctions-related red flags in their business activities (such as geographic location)
- searching for any negative news for any sanctions-related investigations, fines, or judgments in the last five years

Training

Everyone in an organization likely needs basic sanctions knowledge and training. Some employees who encounter sanctions issues regularly may require more detailed training. Your sanctions policy should describe who will receive sanctions training, how often it will be rolled out, how it will be tracked, and who will provide it. Consider US sanctions-specific training for staff in those areas that encounter US business most frequently.

Internal Controls

Internal controls are the processes, procedures, and measures that prevent and detect sanctions violations. Having effective internal controls will reduce your sanctions risks. Your controls will vary depending on your industry, size, global scope, and the results of your risk assessment. However, these are some of the critical controls you will want to implement:

- a written sanctions program
- an economic sanctions policy
- program oversight
- scanning/screening of customers and transactions
- customer and vendor due diligence
- training
- contract language
- risk assessment
- auditing and testing
- written procedures
- environmental scanning

Contract Language

One of the most important tools for staying compliant with sanctions is including exclusion clauses in contracts and insurance policies. These clauses state that the contract or policy is void if a sanctions violation occurs, helping you avoid paying for or covering prohibited transactions. Another clause could forbid the resale of your goods to countries where selling them is banned.

Sanctions exclusion clauses will be discussed in more detail in a subsequent chapter of this guide.

Environmental Scanning

Think of environmental scanning (aka "e-scan") as how you, as the sanctions compliance professional, stay updated on changes in economic sanctions regulations.

Sanctions can change regularly, so you must monitor them daily for changes to the watchlists, updates to sanctions programs, or the implementation of new programs.

Testing and Auditing

Your sanctions program should be reviewed and tested to ensure it operates as expected. This can be done through periodic compliance testing and auditing.

Independent audits check if current processes work effectively and are consistent with the expected procedures and regulatory requirements. They help find weaknesses in the program and recommend ways to fix them.[58] If you regularly do business with a US connection, the group tasked with auditing your program should test for compliance with OFAC in addition to your home jurisdiction.

Compliance testing, on the other hand, involves sample testing the performance of the internal controls to ensure they are functioning effectively.

The Plain-English Guide to Developing an Economic Sanctions Program and its related workbook go into more detail about implementing each of these elements and will assist you in program development with easy-to-use worksheets that cover every step in the process.

8
Scanning/Screening

Most emphasis on complying with sanctions is on scanning, also known as screening. Scanning involves checking a party's name against the sanctions watchlists to see if there is a match. Surprisingly, OFAC does not require anyone to scan their business. However, no compliance program would be effective without it.

What Data Should Be Scanned?

Everyone you do business with should be scanned. This includes:
- all customers (including joint accountholders or multiple insureds under an insurance policy)
- beneficiaries of accounts
- payees to whom checks are issued
- payors who make a payment or deposit on an account
- employees
- vendors
- other business partners, such as attorneys
- third-party claimants (for example, under an auto policy or a loss adjustor)
- joint venture partners
- merger and acquisition targets
- counterparties of trades

If you ship goods, the list of participants who should be scanned is even longer, including:
- purchaser
- seller
- shipper
- shipping company
- vessel name
- consignee
- freight forwarder
- the ultimate beneficiary of the shipment
- countries through which the shipment is transiting

- goods shipped

If you sell high-risk or dual-use goods, you should screen them against their destination to ensure they are not prohibited from being exported there.

Finally, you should also scan countries you are doing business in to know they are not the target of a trade embargo.

OFAC considers an entire transaction prohibited if even one party to it is sanctioned.

How Often Should the Data Be Scanned?

How often and when you scan your data depends on the level of risk involved. For example, a business selling jewelry online might only need to check a customer's name when processing payments. However, companies that manage accounts, like banks or insurers, should screen transactions as they happen and periodically rescan their entire customer list.

In general, OFAC will expect you to scan data **before**:
- onboarding a new customer
- issuing a policy
- sending a payment
- conducting a transaction
- receiving a payment and depositing it into your account
- signing a contract
- renewing a contract or policy
- shipping goods

For businesses managing accounts or contracts, periodic rescans are necessary, even if no transactions have occurred recently, as OFAC prohibits maintaining accounts, contracts, or policies with sanctioned parties.

This doesn't mean you need to screen all your data daily. While OFAC updates its watchlists regularly, it's not a daily occurrence. However, OFAC requires that your watchlists stay up-to-date and that you rescan them immediately after any updates. Most automated systems will update your data within 24 hours of a watchlist change.

If your business involves US-nexus transactions, scan your data on a regular schedule, such as daily (for new customers or payments) and monthly (for continuing accounts or contracts) to meet OFAC's requirements.

Many automated screening systems maintain a customer database. This allows the system to automatically rescan all parties when sanctions lists (like those from the US or UK) are updated. The database is built by storing every scanned item for ongoing monitoring.

How Do We Scan This Data?

The best way to implement sanctions screening is with an automated scanning application. Once it's set up correctly, it requires minimal effort to keep it running. Instead of relying solely on manual scanning—which is time-consuming and prone to mistakes—an automated system lets you focus on reviewing potential matches only rather than sorting through every transaction.

Some companies that offer sanctions screening applications include Lexis Nexis, Moody's, and Computer Services, Inc. (CSI).

If you have multiple systems with data (i.e., customers in one database, payments flowing through another), you'll need to figure out how to extract data from each system to feed through your sanctions screening application. Your IT person should be your initial contact for this task. They'll understand the data that can be extracted, how to do it, and how to format it into a file that can be uploaded and scanned into your sanctions screening application. Most systems allow uploads in Excel, comma-delimited text files, or similar formats.

Larger organizations can arrange real-time scanning by connecting their system, such as a payment system, to the sanctions screening application using an API (Application Programming Interface). This connection instantly checks payee or customer names entered into the system against the sanctions screening application, giving immediate results (match or no match).

Our company set up an internal website with an API that lets employees screen names against a select group of global watchlists. This helped staff quickly check wire payments or new business without sending it to sanctions compliance and waiting for a response, saving time for everyone.

For situations where data cannot be automatically scanned or scanned promptly, manual scanning can be conducted. OFAC offers manual scanning of its lists through the OFAC website: https://sanctionssearch.ofac.treas.gov/.

What Sanctions Lists Should We Use?

OFAC has several watchlists: SDN lists (complete blocking prohibitions) and non-SDN lists (other targeted restrictions). Whenever your transaction has a US nexus, you should ensure your scanning system screens them all.

If you deal in goods (buying, shipping, distributing, or insuring), you must also scan the BIS and DoS lists for parties prohibited from exporting US-origin goods. A consolidated list where you can manually scan all these lists at once is located here: https://www.trade.gov/consolidated-screening-list. Otherwise, most sanctions application vendors will include those lists in their datasets that are available for scanning.

Of course, you should include the foreign government sanctions watchlists for the countries where you do business. Some top picks are Canada, the UK, the EU, and Australia. A data set containing all global sanctions watchlists should be utilized if you do business in every country. Dow Jones has such a list that can be fed as a separate watchlist into your screening solution.

How Should Alerts Be Reviewed?

US-related alerts should be reviewed as soon as possible, as OFAC expects prompt action.

There are a lot of common names on the OFAC lists, so you will likely find a customer who is a name match. . For example, the name "Jose Rodriguez" will produce nine hits at a 100 percent threshold. Are any of these hits positive matches?

Matches are usually determined to be a "false positive" (i.e., not an actual match) after comparing your customer information to the information on the SDN provided by OFAC. Obtain information from your customer, such as middle name, Social Security Number, Date of Birth, and address history, that you can compare to the party on the SDN list to clear this potential match.

Define what criteria you will use to clear an alert. For example, do you rely solely on name, address, and date of birth, or can you use a customer's social media profile picture to estimate their age compared to the sanctioned party? Additionally, specify how many criteria must match to deem it a positive match—name only, name and address, name and date of birth, or all three?

Remember, people move, so not having a match on the address is usually insufficient to clear an alert. You may want to review their address history (obtained from the customer or a public records search such as Lexis Nexis) to verify how long they've lived at certain addresses and whether they've ever lived in the same state or country as the sanctioned party.

You can also search for information on public sites like occupational licenses, home ownership, and property tax records to find information on your customer that can help clear a false positive. News articles showing your sanctioned party operating in a different occupation in a different country from your customer can also help clear a potential match.

If you struggle to clear a match, contact OFAC for guidance. OFAC prefers companies not report matches unless they are confident it's positive. If your customer's information doesn't agree with the SDN details, it's probably safe to clear the alert as a false positive.

The good news for foreign companies is that if you have an OFAC match but, after review, you have no US nexus, then it's likely not business you have to reject or terminate.

Do I Need to Document This?

Yes, keep records of how you confirmed someone isn't a match to the SDN. You might need this information if they show up again as a match or you are asked about it. In my prior role, banks often asked about customers we initiated transactions for who popped up on their sanctions check system. Most automated scanning applications will have space to document your clearing reasons and attach documentation.

Referral Process

However, you cannot rely on scanning alone. Your automated system may not identify all sanctions risks for a transaction.

For example, your customer in the UK has a US bank as a counterparty, and the transaction involves sending goods to Cuba. That data may not appear in your administrative system and may not be sent to your screening application.

Or, an insurance claim occurs in Iranian waters, but your screening system only receives data that shows the customer, the claimant, and the vendors involved in the loss are all non-sanctioned.

That is why a referral process is so important!

Our automated system couldn't catch all the sanctions risks in the policies we wrote, so we set up a referral process for underwriters and claims handlers. For higher-risk policies and claims, we created a straightforward procedure for when and how they should refer cases to the sanctions compliance team. We also trained them on this process and explained why it's crucial. Employee referrals and automated screening are essential parts of a company's sanctions program.

What transactions should you include in your referral program? Consider any risks linked to comprehensively sanctioned countries or higher-risk nations like Russia and Venezuela, where US sanctions differ from other countries' sanctions. Staff will need a clear understanding of what constitutes a sanctions nexus. For the above two examples, the employee setting up the Cuban transaction would refer the business as there is a US bank counterparty, and the claims adjuster would refer the claim as it occurred in Iranian waters.

Best Practice

Consider creating a written sanctions screening program that explains how your automated scanning system works. Include details like which watchlists you use, the threshold for scanning, which data from your administrative systems is scanned, and how often the scanning occurs. This will help you clearly identify which data is being checked against OFAC watchlists, how frequently it's scanned, and whether any data that isn't being scanned should be.

9

What if My Customer Is Sanctioned?

What you need to do if your customer is sanctioned depends on a few factors: whether they are a current or prospective customer, if you hold any assets for them, and which sanctions program they fall under. Some programs restrict only specific activities, not all.

Additionally, you need to determine whether the transaction triggers OFAC involvement (as explained in Chapter 3). You can usually proceed if the transaction doesn't have a US nexus or invoke secondary sanctions. However, since OFAC watchlists often overlap with other countries' watchlists, be sure your customer isn't listed in your jurisdiction before moving forward.

Don't Do Business with Them

For most programs, this will be the first requirement. This means you cannot open an account, issue a policy, sign a contract to provide goods or services, or process a transaction for a party named on the SDN list.

If you already have an account open or active business with them, you must stop working with them immediately. When someone is sanctioned under an OFAC blocking program, you can no longer provide any services to them, including activities that would wind down the business, unless a license is issued (licenses are discussed in Chapter 10). These assets will sit until they expire (in the case of a contract or policy) or get frozen (such as an account with funds in it).

Freeze or Block Assets

When a party is sanctioned under a program requiring an asset freeze, you cannot accept payments or assets from them, make payments to them, or provide other economic resources (such as loans) to them as of the date they are added to the list. OFAC considers any asset owned by an SDN (including cars, townhomes, etc.) to be blocked and cannot be dealt with.

If the asset belongs to the Specially Designated National (SDN), you can't reject the transaction; you must block the assets. Some examples of how this works follow:

- If you receive a loan payment on an account belonging to an SDN, you must retain and block those funds. You can't return them, nor can you apply the payment to their loan balance.
- If you have a payment due to an SDN on a valid insurance claim, again, you can't send the payment, nor can you deny the claim. The claim payment is considered their asset, and you must block it.
- If you are the custodian of an asset belonging to an SDN, such as artwork, you cannot return it.
- If your company holds an insurance policy for an SDN, you can't service it, not even to cancel it.

You will see the terms "blocked" or "frozen" used interchangeably, and they mean the same thing: you cannot release those assets to the SDN.[59] Generally, funds must be put into a bank account blocked by a bank. The account must be interest-bearing, likely prohibiting your company from maintaining the funds in a separate internal account. Maintaining the funds in an internal account and "imputing" interest (i.e., calculating the amount of interest the SDN would receive if the funds were in a bank account) is also inappropriate.

Once the funds are in this blocked bank account, neither you nor the sanctioned party can access them without permission from OFAC. However, the title to the assets remains with the SDN.[60] It is best to contact OFAC for guidance on blocking assets the first time.

Two nuances foreign companies should be aware of when it comes to SDNs with blocked assets:

For foreign companies, you should note that OFAC only requires blocking of assets that are present in the US when blocked, enter the US once blocked, or are in the possession or control of any US person. For example, if a foreign branch of a US company holds assets belonging to an SDN, it is considered a US person and would need to block them.

Also, if a foreign insurance company has an insurance policy with a US nexus, and the insured gets sanctioned by OFAC, the policy is considered a blocked asset. No coverage can be provided and no claims can be paid under it to any party, even a non-sanctioned party. The valid claim will need to sit open until the payment can legally be made or a specific license is requested to pay it.[61] This policy differs from the UK and the EU, which allow processing payments to non-sanctioned parties on a claim where the insured is sanctioned, as they don't technically require policies to be "blocked."

Reject a Transaction

In other programs, rather than freezing assets, there's a prohibition against carrying out a transaction. Some examples of when you would reject a transaction and not freeze the asset include:
- A bank might reject a money transfer to a country like Iran, which is under comprehensive sanctions, since such transactions are forbidden. However, assets are not frozen unless they belong to an SDN.
- A company sends money for a non-sanctioned customer to a sanctioned bank. In this case, the bank's status as an SDN means the transaction should be rejected, but no assets are frozen as the customer is not sanctioned.
- If a prohibited good, like sonar equipment, is being sent to a non-SDN entity in a sanctioned country, you would reject the transaction rather than "freeze" the item.

Report to OFAC

Any time you block assets or reject a transaction due to sanctions, you must file a report within ten business days of the blocking or rejection.[62] There can occasionally be some confusion about when the ten-day clock starts, but we used when the transaction was completed (e.g., the blocked funds entered the blocked bank account), not when the transaction that needed blocking or rejection was initially identified. You can file online at https://ofac.treasury.gov/ofac-reporting-system. Again, it is best to contact OFAC for guidance your first time.

If your company holds blocked assets in a blocked bank account, there is an annual requirement (to be filed by September 30) to report those assets to OFAC. Our bank, which held blocked assets for many different entities, filed the annual report for all its blocked accounts, including ours.

Different countries have different reporting requirements. For example, if you have a match to a US and UK SDN and block assets, you will need to report to both governmental entities. The UK also has an annual reporting requirement.

Case Study

Let's look at an example of how this would work.

You are a German-based company that produces computer chips that contain US parts. These parts give you a US nexus for any transactions related to these chips.

Bob's Tech is a Canadian company that uses those chips in the computers it builds. Bob's Tech becomes an OFAC SDN under a blocking program for selling technology to an entity in Iran.

You cannot sell computer chips to Bob's Tech as they contain US parts (the US nexus), and OFAC sanctioned Bob's Tech.

You cannot use a third party (such as a wholesaler) in another country to sell Bob's Tech the chips. Again, they contain US parts and thus retain their US nexus even in another country. OFAC would consider you to be selling the chips indirectly to Bob's Tech.

You cannot arrange to sell the chips to one of the owners of Bob's Tech, who is not sanctioned. This is considered facilitation and is an OFAC violation.

If Bob's Tech has already sent you payment for the chips, that money must be blocked. The payment cannot be returned to Bob's Tech since he is sanctioned under a blocking program. You cannot deposit them into your own operating account. They must be deposited into a blocked bank account and reported to OFAC.

Your insurance company cannot provide insurance related to any transactions with Bob's Tech (such as product liability). Your bank cannot receive funds or send payments to Bob's Tech.

10
Can I Do Any Business with Sanctioned Parties or Countries?

Even when sanctions are in place against certain parties and countries, OFAC provides legal ways to do business with these parties. They do this through licenses or a non-prohibited transaction.

What Is a License?

A license is permission from OFAC to conduct business normally prohibited by a sanction. There are two types of licenses: general and specific.

OFAC established general licenses that anyone can use for certain transactions. Sometimes, you can conduct your business under a general license.

If no general license is available, you'll need to apply to OFAC for a specific license.[63] A specific license is permission granted by OFAC to a specific party for a particular transaction. Let's take a closer look at these licenses.

General Licenses

OFAC general licenses are available to anyone who believes their activities fit within the terms of the license. You don't need to ask OFAC for permission to use one, and you don't have to tell them you are using it. You can find these licenses on the sanctions program pages under "General Licenses" or in the CFR. General licenses issued outside of the CFR can expire, renew, or be canceled before they expire, but those in the CFR generally don't.

Some general licenses are called "wind-down licenses." They let you keep doing business with a newly sanctioned party briefly while you wrap up your dealings with them. They do not allow you to continue business as usual.

Some activities are licensed under a general license for multiple programs, such as those that cover legal services, work of the US government, or international organizations such as the Red Cross, telecommunications, internet communications, and protecting intellectual property like patents and trademarks.

Jurisdictions such as the UK and the EU also issue general licenses that allow certain activities despite sanctions. However, don't assume that because one country has a general license, OFAC allows the same activity under a general license. Also, the UK can require companies to report using a general license, which OFAC does not.

Below is a discussion of a couple of the more commonly used general licenses.

Humanitarian Aid

The US generally does not prohibit transactions related to humanitarian aid under its sanctions programs, even for countries with trade embargoes.[64]

OFAC has issued general licenses allowing these transactions in most programs and guidance on complying with them.

So, what is considered humanitarian aid?

Generally, these transactions are linked to agriculture, food, medicine, medical devices, and replacement parts. It can also include activities conducted by nonprofit groups that work toward public and social welfare goals or international organizations that benefit the civilian population by meeting basic human needs or building democracy, such as the United Nations World Food Programme.

It is crucial to remember that just because someone says a transaction is for humanitarian reasons, don't rely on it. Not everything fits the definition of humanitarian aid in the sanctions regulations. For instance, some pesticides (generally allowed under the agricultural general license) can't be sent to certain countries, like Russia, because they might be used for chemical weapons. Also, some medical devices need a specific license to export.[65] Plus, these humanitarian licenses usually don't let you transfer funds to a sanctioned party. Always ensure the transaction or item is allowed under the humanitarian license for that program.

Other jurisdictions, such as the UK and the EU, also have humanitarian exceptions in their sanctions programs. However, don't assume all the jurisdictions allow the same activity via their humanitarian licenses.

Personal Remittances

Comprehensive sanctions programs, such as those for Iran, Syria, Cuba, North Korea, and Crimea, permit US individuals to send non-commercial, personal remittances to these countries.[66] General licenses enable financial institutions to process these transactions. With a personal remittance general license, individuals can send money to close relatives in a comprehensively sanctioned area.

However, if the transaction is commercial (e.g., making a purchase or paying an insurance claim), this general license doesn't apply.

For instance, Antonio can send money to his aunt in Cuba without violating US rules. His bank can also process the transfer.

But if Antonio were to die and leave his aunt in Cuba, the proceeds of his life insurance policy, the payment of the claim to the aunt, would be considered a commercial transaction by the insurance company, and the insurer can't use the personal remittance general license to send the funds.

Specific License

A specific license is a written document granted by OFAC to one party for permission to conduct a transaction or series of transactions that would otherwise be prohibited by sanctions.[67] The party that wants a specific license has to apply for it, and OFAC may or may not approve it. Plus, it can take a long time to get one approved. Only parties covered under the specific license can use it.

When applying for the license, request coverage for all third parties involved in the transaction. This could include insurance companies handling claims, third-party providers hired for assistance, and banks handling payments. Otherwise, each organization involved in the transaction may need a separate license to participate. Just because someone you are doing business with has a license doesn't mean your company does, unless you are listed in the license.

In addition, having a Bureau of Industry and Security (BIS) license to export a specific good doesn't eliminate the need for an OFAC license if OFAC otherwise prohibits the transaction. Likewise, if you have an OFAC license for the good, be aware that you may or may not also need a BIS license to export it.

In my prior position, we used specific licenses to make payments on claims that would otherwise be prohibited due to sanctions. For example, a maritime incident occurred in Crimean waters, a comprehensively sanctioned jurisdiction. The specific license obtained by the customer allowed the issuance of claims payments and the hiring of third parties to conduct salvage, among other services.

Non-Prohibited Transactions

As mentioned before, depending on the program someone is sanctioned under, you may still be able to do business with them, just not the prohibited activity. This occurs most with parties sanctioned under Non-SDN list programs. If you identify a customer or other party as a positive match, review the program under which they are sanctioned to see what is prohibited.

For example, suppose a foreign branch of a US entity wants to purchase a product from a company in China. You search the OFAC list and find out they are sanctioned under the Non-SDN Chinese Military-Industrial Complex Companies List. This program prohibits the purchase of public securities of certain Chinese companies due to their ties to the Chinese military. However, it allows other types of transactions, such as purchasing goods.[68] In this example, you can proceed with your transaction, as the prohibitions of this sanctions program do not apply to your purchase.

Our company had a Hong Kong office with many Chinese customers, some of whom were on this list. However, the insurance we provided was not considered the purchase of public securities, so we could offer the insurance.

Guidance and Frequently Asked Questions (FAQs)

I've discussed reviewing different sources, such as Executive Orders, Directives, general licenses, and the CFR, to see if you can do business with someone. Two additional sources to review that may assist you in deciding if your transaction is allowed are guidance and FAQs.

OFAC sometimes issues guidance on topics like complying with humanitarian general licenses and providing legal help to sanctioned parties. They have also issued over one thousand FAQs that answer common questions about their rules. These FAQs cover everything from what OFAC does to specifics about what you can and can't do under different sanctions programs or with newly sanctioned parties.

But remember, guidance and FAQs are not the same as licenses or regulations; they don't have the force of law. Instead, they are more like this guide, helping you understand and comply with sanctions. Interpretations can and do change over time, so staying updated and consulting with internal or external legal counsel when needed is essential.

11
Legal Considerations

One of the most important tools for staying compliant with sanctions is including exclusion clauses in contracts and insurance policies. These clauses state that the contract or policy is void if a sanctions violation occurs, helping you avoid paying for or covering prohibited transactions. Another clause could forbid the resale of your goods to countries where selling them is banned.

OFAC said, "The best and most reliable approach for insuring global risks without violating US sanctions law is to insert in global insurance policies an explicit exclusion for risks that would violate US sanctions law... It essentially shifts the risk of loss for the underlying transaction back to the insured - the person more likely to have direct control over the economic activity giving rise to the contact with a sanctioned country, entity, or individual."[69]

In reality, you must not engage in any transaction that violates economic sanctions, even if that's not explicitly stated in your contract. However, including such a clause can offer you legal protection in a dispute, provide a basis for OFAC to reduce fines, and notify the contracted party that they won't be covered in situations where sanctions are violated.

You will want to enlist an attorney to ensure your sanctions clauses are valid and well-worded to protect you.

Sanctions exclusion language should be consistent across all documents and contracts to prevent gaps or discrepancies. You may want to include the approved exclusion language in your economic sanctions policy to ensure consistency.

We based our sanctions exclusion language on Lloyd's LMA3100 form.[70] Lloyd's sanctions exclusion language is widely accepted. The language states that the insurer isn't liable for any claim and is not required to provide any coverage under the policy to the extent that it would expose the insurer to sanctions.

When contracting with a vendor for services, ensure the contract mandates compliance with sanctions and that they cannot become sanctioned, or payment will not be made under the contract. Consider adding language requiring them to report any sanctions violations to you as part of your ongoing vendor monitoring process.

Similarly, if goods are sold to a third party, like a wholesaler, the contract should specify that the goods cannot be resold in a way that breaches sanctions, such as selling to a sanctioned party or country.

If your contract or the contract participants cover multiple jurisdictions, the sanctions exclusion clause should clearly list the regions where a sanctions violation would void the contract. Typically, your sanctions exclusion clause would state that the contract becomes invalid if it breaches laws in any of these jurisdictions: your own, the contractor's, and the jurisdiction(s) where the transactions are conducted. Specifying these countries ensures there's no debate about invoking the sanctions clause if an OFAC violation occurs.

Clarifying which legal jurisdiction governs your contract is crucial because sanctions regulations vary between jurisdictions, affecting what's permissible. For instance, if you're under UK jurisdiction and the transaction could breach US but not UK sanctions, you wouldn't want a clause that only covers compliance with UK sanctions regulations.

UK/EU Blocking Statutes

Be aware, however, that sanctions clauses may not fully protect you in legal disputes, and a European company attempting to comply with OFAC sanctions as well as its own is like navigating a minefield.

The EU and the UK have "blocking statutes"[71] barring compliance with OFAC sanctions that conflict with their own (such as those for Iran and Cuba). This aims to protect UK and EU companies from extraterritorial laws and allow them to conduct business freely.

While the UK and EU governments won't sue companies for invoking a sanctions clause, affected companies can bring civil cases against them.

Recent court cases have shown mixed outcomes.

In 2018, the UK High Court ruled insurers aren't liable to pay a claim when payments violate sanctions laws.[72] The Court said the blocking statute did not apply as the sanctions exclusion clause was part of the contract, not a direct response to US sanctions laws.[73]

In 2019, the UK High Court sided with a defendant who refused to make a payment to an OFAC-sanctioned party. The court stated that the policy clearly outlined sanctions compliance, and the plaintiff should have been aware of the risks.[74]

In 2020, a UK bank stopped making interest payments to a lender in Cyprus because the lender's owner had become an OFAC SDN. As a result, the lender was considered sanctioned under the 50 Percent Rule, and the bank was worried about facing US secondary sanctions. The defendant used a nonpayment clause in the facility agreement to justify this action. The English Court of Appeal decided that the bank could rely on this nonpayment clause because US secondary sanctions were considered a "mandatory provision of law," as stated in the clause. In this case, the risk of breaching US secondary sanctions was enough to enforce the clause.[75]

However, in 2021, the EU Court of Justice ruled that companies under EU jurisdiction can't take action solely to comply with US sanctions if it violates the EU's blocking statute. The company must prove it wasn't seeking to comply with US sanctions laws when it canceled the business but took action for another appropriate reason.[76]

While this section focused on EU and UK blocking statutes, be aware that other countries such as China, Canada, France, and Germany also have blocking statutes. Their enforcement of these statutes may differ from that of the UK and EU.

To protect your company from blocking statutes, consider:
- Excluding certain jurisdictions in your contracts. Add territorial exclusion clauses in your contracts to avoid transactions in places like Iran or Cuba, alongside sanctions exclusion clauses. This is particularly important if you are a foreign company and the transaction could have a US nexus.
- Relying on other contract clauses. Use general non-compliance with laws and regulations clauses or other legal grounds for ending a contract instead of citing sanctions.
- Carefully documenting your business decisions when canceling business due to sanctions. The documentation must show solid reasons for terminating a business, and these reasons must not show an intention to comply with US laws.

- Applying for a specific OFAC license. You might consider applying for an OFAC license to conduct the transaction. However, you must first get permission (i.e., a license) from the UK or EU authority to apply for an OFAC license, and these applications are public. If your customer sees you're trying to comply with US sanctions that conflict with UK or EU sanctions, it might sue you.

So, sanctions clauses can help your company avoid violations of OFAC sanctions and the associated fines, but they may not fully protect against lawsuits under other countries' blocking statutes.

12
Managing US Parent Versus Foreign Branch or Subsidiary Conflicts

Global companies sometimes face disagreements between their US headquarters and foreign branches or subsidiaries about whether to take on particular business. The US parent company might be cautious about approving business that's legal for the foreign office but could lead to future sanctions or reputational problems. On the other hand, the foreign office might want to pursue business even if the US parent company believes it could violate sanctions. In its enforcement release for AL Middle East, OFAC said: "Non-US companies should be aware of how their activities might trigger compliance issues with US sanctions, including when they place orders with US affiliates or subsidiaries."[77]

Resolving these conflicts can be challenging due to legal and regulatory barriers and can lead to tension between legal/compliance and foreign business units, especially when the business comes from VIP customers or offers a high income. Executives may push back against compliance advice to reject the business.

So, can these conflicts be resolved or at least managed?

Ultimately, if the company proceeds with business that appears to be prohibited by OFAC, you will need to decide whether to self-report the violation to reduce a future OFAC penalty. They might also choose to write business that you know, based on your deep understanding of current sanctions, will eventually be prohibited, creating more work to unwind later. You will have to monitor that business carefully so you can take action if and when a sanction occurs.

OFAC has fined many companies for violations their foreign subsidiaries or branches incurred, some of which conducted the transaction after the US parent company told them to cease that activity. One example is Black and Decker, which OFAC fined because its Chinese subsidiary exported or tried to export tools to Iran.[78]

The following are two potential solutions we utilized to manage these conflicts.

Risk Decision Matrix

Documenting the decision-making process in a risk decision matrix could be valuable. It shows who in the company is responsible for decisions on sanctions-related issues. My prior organization had one, and we often referred to it during challenging discussions about policies or claims with a sanctions nexus. Our matrix was simply an Excel spreadsheet with five levels of decision-making depending on the situation.

Tier 1: Business line staff make the decisions. No sanctions issue exists, so the employees conduct business as usual.

Tier 2: The sanctions compliance team makes the decision. Someone on the sanctions team can resolve a potential sanctions issue, such as clearing a false positive match.

Tier 3: The SCO or the sanctions compliance team manager decides. Potential business that may violate sanctions is escalated to the manager or the SCO. They can decline the business if a transaction or account violates sanctions. Otherwise, if necessary, they can resolve the issue with input from other company staff.

Tier 4: Business line management makes the decision. Usually, these decisions are risk-related. The customer or transaction is at high risk for a potential sanctions violation, so the decision is whether to accept the customer or conduct the transaction. Business line management has the final say, although the SCO and legal counsel may provide their input during decision-making. This tier is not for transactions that clearly violate sanctions; that decision rests in Tier 3 with sanctions compliance staff.

Tier 5: Senior management participates in the decision. A sanctions violation may have occurred, so executive management determines the response (such as self-reporting to OFAC) with input from the SCO, legal counsel, and business line staff.

Recusal Policy

Another way to manage these conflicts is by implementing an internal recusal policy. If your foreign subsidiary is legally allowed to write business that your US entity cannot, the transaction may be able to proceed as long as all US involvement is avoided, including any participation from US staff (i.e., a US nexus is avoided).

For example, your subsidiary has an opportunity to write a policy that involves the Venezuelan government, an OFAC-sanctioned group. If there is no other US nexus (no US parties involved in the policy, it's not denominated in US dollars, and transactions don't include US financial institutions, for example), then the business may be allowable if a recusal policy is followed.

We established a recusal policy where US employees, such as underwriters, claims adjusters, and managers, were excluded from participating in specific policies and claims throughout their duration. The potential business was referred to the sanctions compliance team for review, which informed the foreign subsidiary that US employees couldn't participate in that policy or claim.

However, this won't work in situations involving Iran or Cuba since foreign subsidiaries are US persons under those regulations.

One exception to recusal is that US employees can still offer legal and compliance advice to their foreign counterparts on complying with US sanctions and whether OFAC prohibits a transaction.[79]

If you institute a recusal policy, be careful that no US person gets involved in negotiating, handling, or decision-making on the activity. OFAC fined one company because US senior managers approved contracts for a foreign subsidiary, violating Directive 4 of the Ukraine-/Russia-related Sanctions.[80] This fine may not have occurred if a recusal policy had been properly followed.

13
Penalties for Non-Compliance

OFAC is responsible for the civil enforcement of US sanctions laws and regulations. Violations can result in substantial fines, and civil and criminal penalties can exceed several million dollars.[81] Other governmental agencies, such as the Department of Justice (DOJ) or the New York Department of Financial Services, can also impose their own penalties for the same conduct. Throughout this guide, I've noted several instances where foreign companies have been penalized by OFAC. Below are a couple larger fines that illustrate the extent to which a company may be subject to penalties.

British American Tobacco (BAT) settled with OFAC for $508 million for violations of the weapons proliferation and North Korea sanctions regulations. BAT is UK-based, and its foreign subsidiary in Singapore was also involved in these transactions, so they weren't automatically US persons for purposes of these regulations. However, the transactions had a US nexus, specifically using a US correspondent banking account and a foreign branch of a US bank to clear these transactions.[82]

The largest fine to date happened in November 2023, totaling $968 million, against Binance. Binance got in trouble for not setting up systems to spot and report suspicious transactions involving terrorists, ransomware gangs, money launderers, and other criminals. OFAC said Binance purposely undermined and ineffectually implemented its own sanctions compliance controls.[83]

Besides fines, employees, officers, and directors face severe consequences like losing their jobs or going to jail. The DOJ and the US Attorney might bring criminal charges. For instance, in 2022, a US citizen was sentenced to more than five years in prison. He violated sanctions laws by helping North Korea use blockchain and cryptocurrency to hide money and avoid US sanctions.[84]

It is important to note that OFAC operates on a strict liability basis. This means you can be fined for a violation of any amount (in theory, one dollar), even if you did not intend to violate sanctions. However, penalties will depend, in part, on the amount of the violation, whether it was inadvertent or deliberate, and whether you identified and reported the breach to OFAC.

You can significantly lower the fine if you self-report an identified violation to OFAC. OFAC considers non-reporting to be an aggravating factor that could increase your penalty. Binance, for example, did not self-report the violations to OFAC.

And again, don't overlook the damage to your reputation and your company's reputation when OFAC releases a press statement about your violation. Bad publicity and all the negative fallout from that violation can hurt your finances even more. Banks and customers might use this negative news to decide whether to work with you.

14
Conclusion

In the ever-evolving landscape of global commerce, navigating economic sanctions can be complex. Staying informed about OFAC economic sanctions is crucial for foreign companies and their employees. These sanctions can significantly impact your business, and failure to comply may lead to costly penalties and harm your company's reputation. Participating in the US marketplace is vital for many foreign entities, making compliance even more critical.

Sanctions are constantly evolving, which makes it challenging for foreign businesses that don't deal with US sanctions daily. New programs and watchlists are regularly introduced or updated, meaning what's permissible today may not be tomorrow. This guide, along with other available resources, can help you stay up-to-date and ensure your business remains compliant.

Compliance isn't just about avoiding fines—it's about upholding ethical and legal standards in an increasingly complex global landscape. By following sanctions regulations, your organization contributes to international stability and security and fosters trust within your industry. Being proactive will help you navigate this challenging environment with confidence.

With the knowledge and strategies outlined in this guide, you now have the tools to manage sanctions risks effectively and ensure compliance with regulations set forth by the Office of Foreign Assets Control (OFAC).

15
Test Your Knowledge

Now, it is time to test your knowledge of the concepts presented in this guide.

Questions

1. You work for a foreign branch of a US-based company that wants to sign a contract to sell products to the Government of Venezuela. Can you do this business?
    a. Would your answer change if you worked for the foreign subsidiary of the US-based company?

2. You are a US branch of an Indian company. Your customer wants to sell your sonar equipment to a party in Russia. You recognize that OFAC regulations prohibit exporting this equipment to Russia. Are any of your responses below appropriate?
    a. Refer the business to your parent company in India, as they may be able to make the sale.
    b. Complete the transaction using a wholesaler in China, which does not prohibit the export of your sonar equipment to Russia.
    c. Decline the business as you are considered a US person, and this is a violation of OFAC.

3. You are a foreign branch of a US-based company that wants to do business with A Russian Company, an entity on the Sectoral Sanctions Identifications (SSI) list. Can you do this business?
    a. No. They are sanctioned, so we can't do the business.
    b. Possibly, depending on the business we want to do with them.
    c. Yes. The sectoral sanctions list is a non-SDN list, so we can do the business.

4. You are a foreign entity with a new business consultant, Jose Morales, in Canada, who will generate some business for you in North America. Do you need to scan this person against the OFAC lists?
    a. Yes.
    b. No. He's Canadian.

5. Your foreign insurance company is asked to provide insurance to Oligarch Property Management, which has UK and US townhomes. The management company is listed as the owner of the properties. You scan the management company, and it is not sanctioned. However, you learn by talking to one of the employees that the beneficial owner of the properties is a Russian person. When you scan the name, you discover he is sanctioned by OFAC and the UK. Can you provide this insurance?
   a. No. A sanctioned party is the beneficial owner of the property.
   b. Yes. Our customer is the management company, which isn't sanctioned.

6. You work for a foreign branch of a US-based accounting firm. Your branch wants to do business with XYZ Company, a Russian energy company. You scan XYZ Company, and they are not on the SDN list. Are you clear to do business with them?
   a. No
   b. Yes
   c. Not yet

7. A Canadian firm with a branch in Russia wants your US-based insurance company to provide liability insurance to its entire organization. The Russian branch is sanctioned by OFAC. Are any of the following responses appropriate?
   a. You can't issue the policy through your US writing company, but refer it to your UK subsidiary to write.
   b. You can write the policy if there is a territorial exclusion for Russia and the Russian branch.
   c. You can't issue the policy because one of the branches is sanctioned, which means the entire organization is sanctioned.

8. You work for a foreign company that is not considered a US person. You are conducting a sale of your video games to a company in Syria. After completing the transaction, you discovered that you sent payment through a foreign bank that used a US correspondent account to complete the transaction. What do you do?

a. This is likely a violation of OFAC as a US financial institution was used during the sales process. Discuss with management whether to self-report this violation to OFAC.

b. Do nothing. There is no OFAC violation to this transaction. You sent the transaction through a foreign bank, not the US correspondent bank.

9. You work for a foreign financial institution with no US ties that has a Russian aerospace customer. Do you have an OFAC issue with this account?

a. No. There is no US nexus.

b. Yes. This could be a violation of OFAC's secondary sanctions.

10. Your company is a freight forwarder located in Germany facilitating a shipment of medical supplies from the US to India. You scan all parties involved in the shipment and discover the vessel is sanctioned. Can you conduct this shipment?

a. No. A party to the shipment is sanctioned, so the entire transaction is prohibited.

b. Yes. Our customer is not sanctioned.

c. Yes. It involves medical supplies, which fall under a humanitarian general license.

Answers

1. No. The Government of Venezuela is sanctioned by OFAC. As the foreign branch of a US company, you are considered a US person.
   a. Maybe. The foreign subsidiary may be able to do this business as it is not subject to OFAC regulations. However, verify there is no US nexus to the transaction and implement a recusal policy for US personnel.

2. C. You must decline the business as you are considered a US person, and this transaction would violate OFAC. Referring the business to your parent company in India (choice A) is considered facilitation by OFAC and is illegal. Remember, US persons are not allowed to refer business to another company that they themselves cannot conduct. Completing the transaction using a wholesaler in China (choice C) would indirectly supply the goods to Russia, which OFAC also considers a sanctions violation.

3. B. Depending on the business you want to do with them, you may be able to conduct it since OFAC's SSI list is a non-SDN list, and only certain activities are prohibited. If you want to sell A Russian Company computer parts, it will likely be a prohibited transaction that you cannot conduct. If, instead, you want to import grain from Russia, that will likely be allowed.

4. A. You have to scan a new business partner who may be generating US-related business for you through OFAC, no matter where they are located, as OFAC can sanction anyone anywhere in the world.

5. A. The beneficial owner of the townhome you are asked to insure is sanctioned. The townhome is "frozen" by its sanctioned ownership, and you can't provide services, such as insurance, for it.

6. C. Knowing they are a Russian company and that the US has prohibited providing accounting services to entities within Russia, you likely cannot provide the service. However, there are exceptions to review first. Would the services be provided to a subsidiary in another country? Is the Russian entity owned or controlled by a US person? In those situations, you may be able to provide the service.

7. B is the best response. As long as that sanctioned branch is excluded from coverage, you should be able to insure the rest of the company. Referring a firm to your subsidiary that may be able to provide a service you cannot due to OFAC sanctions could be considered facilitation (choice A), and the entire company is not sanctioned just by virtue of a branch being sanctioned (choice C).

8. A. This is likely an OFAC violation. The fact that the payment went through a US correspondent bank account, even though your company did not send it through the account directly, still gave the transaction a US nexus, and most transactions with Syria are prohibited.

9. B. Being a foreign financial institution (FFI) with an account for a Russian aerospace company could violate Executive Order 14024, which imposes secondary sanctions on FFIs doing business with Russian SDNs in specific industries and any persons operating in certain sectors, such as aerospace. You should consider divesting yourself of that account.

10. A. A party to the transaction (in this case, the vessel) is sanctioned by OFAC, so the entire transaction is prohibited. Just because your customer is not sanctioned (choice B) doesn't mean the transaction is legal. A humanitarian general license (choice C) is not applicable as India, the ultimate destination, is not a sanctioned jurisdiction and has no general licenses available. However, you can continue the shipment if you use a non-sanctioned vessel.

References

Below is a good reference list of websites with further details on the information provided in this guide.

All OFAC Sanctions Programs
https://ofac.treasury.gov/sanctions-programs-and-country-information

OFAC Frequently Asked Questions
https://ofac.treasury.gov/faqs/all-faqs

Free OFAC List Search Tool
https://sanctionssearch.ofac.treas.gov/

OFAC Compliance Guidance for Sanctions Programs
https://ofac.treasury.gov/media/16331/download?inline

UK Sanctions Programs
https://www.gov.uk/government/collections/financial-sanctions-regime-specific-consolidated-lists-and-releases

EU Sanctions Programs
https://www.sanctionsmap.eu/#/main

OFAC Enforcement Actions
https://ofac.treasury.gov/civil-penalties-and-enforcement-information

Department of Commerce, Department of the Treasury, and Department of Justice Tri-Seal Compliance Note: Obligations of foreign-based persons to comply with US sanctions and export control laws
https://www.justice.gov/opa/media/1341411/dl?inline

Bureau of Industry and Security Lists of Parties of Concern
https://www.bis.doc.gov/index.php/policy-guidance/lists-of-parties-of-concern/entity-list

US Department of State, Directorate of Defense Trade Controls
https://www.pmddtc.state.gov/ddtc_public/ddtc_public

US Department of State, Bureau of International Security and Nonproliferation https://www.state.gov/bureaus-offices/under-secretary-for-arms-control-and-international-security-affairs/bureau-of-international-security-and-nonproliferation/

Consolidated Screening List
https://www.trade.gov/consolidated-screening-list

United Nations Sanctions
https://main.un.org/securitycouncil/en/sanctions/information

Author Biography

Heidi Hunter worked for a US-based insurance company with global operations for over a decade. She developed and managed the company's sanctions compliance program, covering all its locations. She oversaw the team responsible for complying with sanctions and worked closely with other teams within the company to ensure they understood and followed sanctions regulations. Heidi has a Master of Business Administration (MBA) and is a Certified Public Accountant (inactive).

Visit her website at https://easysanctions.wordpress.com/ for more information on sanctions and to sign up for her newsletter.

All Books in the Plain-English Guide Series by Heidi Hunter

The Plain-English Guide to Economic Sanctions

The Plain-English Guide to Developing an Economic Sanctions Program

The Plain-English Guide to Economic Sanctions Risk Assessments

The Plain-English Guide to Economic Sanctions for Insurance Companies

The Plain-English Guide to Economic Sanctions for Foreign Companies

The Plain-English Guide to Economic Sanctions: The Complete Series

Companion Workbooks:

The Plain-English Guide to Developing an Economic Sanctions Program Workbook

The Plain-English Guide to Economic Sanctions Risk Assessments Workbook

Find them all at: https://easysanctions.wordpress.com/books/

If you read one of my guides, please post a rating or review!

Notes

1. Due to the end of Bashar al-Assad's regime, on January 6, 2025, OFAC issued General License 24, expanding authorizations for activities and transactions in Syria for an initial six-month period, effective until July 7, 2025. This may lead to the permanent loosening of comprehensive sanctions against Syria.

2. OFAC, Frequently Asked Questions, FAQ 986, https://ofac.treasury.gov/faqs/all-faqs.

3. OFAC, FAQ 18.

4. OFAC, FAQ 3.

5. OFAC, FAQ 3.

6. European Union Sanctions, https://www.eeas.europa.eu/eeas/european-union-sanctions_en.

7. Edward J. Collins-Chase, "Sanctions Primer: How the United States Uses Restrictive Mechanisms to Advance Foreign Policy or National Security Objectives" (Congressional Research Service, 2023), https://crsreports.congress.gov/product/pdf/R/R47829.

8. OFAC, Russian Harmful Foreign Activities Sanctions page, https://ofac.treasury.gov/sanctions-programs-and-country-information/russian-harmful-foreign-activities-sanctions.

9. *Code of Federal Regulations*, Title 31, Subpart B, Chapter V, Part 549 Lebanese Sanctions Regulations, https://www.ecfr.gov/current/title-31/subtitle-B/chapter-V/part-549?toc=1.

10. OFAC, Afghanistan-Related Sanctions page, https://ofac.treasury.gov/sanctions-programs-and-country-information/afghanistan-related-sanctions.

11. OFAC, FAQ 886.

12. OFAC, FAQ 10.

13. Wilkie Compliance, "Overview of US Sanctions," accessed April 25, 2024, https://complianceconcourse.willkie.com/resources/sanctions-us-overview-of-us-sanctions/.

14. Edward J. Collins-Chase.

15. *Code of Federal Regulations*, Global Magnitsky Sanctions Regulations, 31 CFR Part 583, https://www.ecfr.gov/current/title-31/subtitle-B/chapter-V/part-583/subpart-B/section-583.201.

16. *Code of Federal Regulations*, Global Magnitsky Sanctions Regulations.

17. OFAC, Other OFAC Sanctions Lists, https://ofac.treasury.gov/other-ofac-sanctions-lists; OFAC, FAQ 91.

18. OFAC, Ukraine-/Russia-related Sanctions, https://ofac.treasury.gov/sanctions-programs-and-country-information/ukraine-russia-related-sanctions.

19. OFAC, "Directive 1 (As Amended on September 29, 2017) Under Executive Order 13662", https://ofac.treasury.gov/media/8696/download?inline.

20. OFAC, Other Lists, Non-SDN Menu Based Sanctions List, https://ofac.treasury.gov/other-ofac-sanctions-lists.

21. Executive Order 14059 of December 15, 2021, "Imposing Sanctions on Foreign Persons Involved in the Global Illicit Drug Trade," https://ofac.treasury.gov/media/917361/download?inline.

22. OFAC, "Determination Pursuant to Section 1(A)(Ii) of Executive Order 14024," https://ofac.treasury.gov/media/926586/download?inline.

23. OFAC, "Determination Pursuant to Section 1(a)(i) of Executive Order 14024," May 8, 2022, https://ofac.treasury.gov/media/922951/download?inline; OFAC, FAQ 1061.

24. OFAC, "Determination Pursuant To Section 1(A)(ii) of Executive Order 14071, Prohibitions Related to Certain Quantum Computing Services," https://ofac.treasury.gov/media/926591/download?inline.

25. OFAC, FAQ 1061.

26. Executive Order 14068, "Prohibiting Certain Imports, Exports, and New Investment with Respect to Continued Russian Federation Aggression," March 11, 2022, https://ofac.treasury.gov/media/919281/download?inline.

27. Executive Order 14066, "Prohibiting Certain Imports and New Investments with Respect to Continued Russian Federation Efforts To

Undermine the Sovereignty and Territorial Integrity of Ukraine," March 8, 2022, https://ofac.treasury.gov/media/919111/download?inline.

28. OFAC, Determination Pursuant to Section 1(a)(i)(A) of Executive Order 14068, "Prohibitions Related to Imports of Aluminum, Copper, and Nickel of Russian Federation Origin," https://ofac.treasury.gov/media/932796/download?inline.

29. Bureau of Industry and Security, Common High Priority List, https://www.bis.gov/articles/russia-export-controls-list-common-high-priority-items.

30. OFAC, FAQ 91.

31. Executive Order 13884, "Blocking Property of the Government of Venezuela," August 5, 2019, https://ofac.treasury.gov/media/26786/download?inline.

32. OFAC, FAQ 91.

33. Department of the Treasury, "Revised Guidance on Entities Owned by Persons Whose Property and Interests in Property Are Blocked," https://ofac.treasury.gov/media/6186/download?inline; OFAC, FAQ 399.

34. Scott Patterson and Ian Talley, "Sanctioned Russian Oligarch Deripaska Distances Himself From Rusal", *Wall Street Journal,* April 27, 2018, https://www.wsj.com/articles/russian-tycoon-oleg-deripaska-to-sell-majority-stake-in-en-group-1524848098.

35. OFAC, FAQ 11.

36. *Code of Federal Regulations*, Cuban Asset Control Regulations, 31 CFR§ 515.329, https://www.ecfr.gov/current/title-31/subtitle-B/chapter-V/part-515?toc=1.

37. *Code of Federal Regulations*, Iranian Transactions and Sanctions Regulations, 31 CFR§ 560.215, https://www.ecfr.gov/current/title-31/subtitle-B/chapter-V/part-560?toc=1.

38. *Code of Federal Regulations*, "North Korea Sanctions Regulations," 31 C.F.R. §510.214, https://www.ecfr.gov/current/title-31/subtitle-B/chapter-V/part-510/subpart-B/section-510.214.

39. OFAC, "OFAC Settles with Swedbank Latvia for $3,430,900 Related to Apparent Violations of Sanctions on Crimea," June 26, 2023, https://ofac.treasury.gov/media/931911/download?inline.

40. OFAC, "OFAC Settles with Toll Holdings Limited for $6,131,855 Related to Apparent Violations of Multiple Sanctions Programs," April 25, 2022, https://ofac.treasury.gov/media/922441/download?inline.

41. Dow Jones, "What are Secondary Sanctions?" Dow Jones Risk & Compliance Glossary, accessed April 25, 2024, https://www.dowjones.com/professional/risk/glossary/sanctions/secondary-sanctions/.

42. OFAC, "Re-Imposition of the Sanctions on Iran That Had Been Lifted or Waived Under the JCPOA," November 4, 2018, https://ofac.treasury.gov/sanctions-programs-and-country-information/iran-sanctions/re-imposition-of-the-sanctions-on-iran-that-had-been-lifted-or-waived-under-the-jcpoa.

43. Executive Order 14114, "Taking Additional Steps with Respect to the Russian Federation's Harmful Activities," December 22, 2023, https://ofac.treasury.gov/media/932441/download?inline.

44. OFAC "Treasury Sanctions Investors Supporting Assad Regime's Corrupt Reconstruction Efforts," June 17, 2020, https://home.treasury.gov/news/press-releases/sm1037 (Nader Kalai and Luxury Tourism Section).

45. *Code of Federal Regulations*, Iraq Stabilization and Insurgency Sanctions Regulations, § 576.315, https://www.ecfr.gov/current/title-31/subtitle-B/chapter-V/part-576/subpart-C/section-576.315.

46. OFAC, "Alfa Laval Middle East Ltd. Settles Potential Civil Liability for Apparent Violations of the Iranian Transactions and Sanctions Regulations," July 19, 2021, https://ofac.treasury.gov/media/911521/download?inline.

47. *Code of Federal Regulations*, § 560.208, Iranian Transactions and Sanctions Regulations, Prohibited Facilitation by United States Persons of Transactions by Foreign Persons, https://www.ecfr.gov/current/title-31/subtitle-B/chapter-V/part-560/subpart-B/section-560.208.

48. OFAC, "Alfa Laval Inc Settles Potential Civil Liability for Apparent Violations of the Iranian Transactions and Sanctions Regulations," July 19, 2021, https://ofac.treasury.gov/media/911516/download?inline.

49. Department of Commerce, Department of the Treasury, and Department of Justice, "Tri-Seal Compliance Note: Obligations of foreign-

based persons to comply with US sanctions and export control laws," March 6, 2024, https://www.justice.gov/opa/media/1341411/dl?inline.

50. OFAC, "CSE Global Limited and CSE TransTel Pte. Ltd. Settle Potential Civil Liability for Apparent Violations of the International Emergency Economic Powers Act and the Iranian Transactions and Sanctions Regulations," July 27, 2017, https://ofac.treasury.gov/media/11186/download?inline.

51. EU Council Regulation (E.C.) No 2271/96 of November 22, 1996, as amended by Commission Delegated Regulation (E.U.) 2018/1100 of June 6, 2018, https://www.legislation.gov.uk/eur/1996/2271; "Spotlight on the U.K. Protection of Trading Interests Legislation," Wilkie Compliance, accessed April 25, 2024, https://complianceconcourse.willkie.com/resources/sanctions-uk-uk-blocking-statute/.

52. Department of Commerce, Department of the Treasury, and Department of Justice, "Tri-Seal Compliance Note."

53. Department of Commerce, Department of the Treasury, and Department of Justice, "Tri-Seal Compliance Note."

54. OFAC, "Alcon Laboratories, Inc., Alcon Pharmaceuticals Ltd., and Alcon Management, SA, Settle Potential Civil Liability for Apparent Violations of the Iranian Transactions and Sanctions Regulations and the Sudanese Sanctions Regulations," July 5, 2016, https://ofac.treasury.gov/media/11641/download?inline.

55. US Department of State, Directorate of Defense Trade Controls, Defense Trade Controls Compliance (DTCC), accessed on October 27, 2024, https://www.pmddtc.state.gov/ddtc_public/ddtc_public?id=ddtc_kb_article_page&sys_id=000d7b84dbc7bf0044f9ff621f9619a3.

56. US Department of State, Bureau of International Security and Nonproliferation, accessed on October 27, 2024, https://www.state.gov/bureaus-offices/under-secretary-for-arms-control-and-international-security-affairs/bureau-of-international-security-and-nonproliferation/.

57. Department of the Treasury, "A Framework for OFAC Compliance Commitments," https://ofac.treasury.gov/media/16331/download?inline.

58. Department of the Treasury, "A Framework for OFAC Compliance Commitments."

59. OFAC, FAQ 9.

60. OFAC, FAQ 9.

61 OFAC, FAQ 63.

62. OFAC, FAQ 49.

63. OFAC, FAQ 8.

64. OFAC, "Supplemental Guidance for The Provision of Humanitarian Assistance," February 27, 2023, https://ofac.treasury.gov/media/931341/download?inline; FAQ 1105.

65. OFAC, "United Medical Instruments Inc. Settles Potential Civil Liability for Alleged Violations of the Iranian Transactions and Sanctions Regulations," February 28, 2017, https://ofac.treasury.gov/media/11181/download?inline.

66. OFAC, FAQs 227, 243, 453, 462, 732.

67. OFAC, FAQ 74.

68. OFAC, FAQ 905.

69. OFAC, FAQ 102.

70. Lloyds Market Association Bulletin LMA23-028-AR, "Sanctions Clauses," October 5, 2023, https://www.lmalloyds.com/LMA_Bulletins/LMA23-028-AR.aspx.

71. EU Council Regulation (E.C.) No 2271/96 of November 22, 1996, as amended by Commission Delegated Regulation (E.U.) 2018/1100 of June 6, 2018, https://www.legislation.gov.uk/eur/1996/2271; "Spotlight on the U.K. Protection of Trading Interests Legislation," Wilkie Compliance, accessed April 25, 2024, https://complianceconcourse.willkie.com/resources/sanctions-uk-uk-blocking-statute/.

72. Debevoise and Plimpton, "UK High Court Rules on Sanctions Clauses in Insurance Contracts and Considers Application of the EU Blocking Regulation," October 30, 2018, https://www.debevoise.com/-/media/files/insights/publications/-2018/10/20181030_uk_high_court_rules_on_sanctions_clauses_in_insurance_contracts_and_considers_application_of_the_eu_blocking_regulation.pdf.

73. Debevoise and Plimpton.

74. Baker McKenzie, "Sanctions clauses and US extraterritorial sanctions – Lamesa v Cynergy appeal," July 10, 2020, https://sanctionsnews.bakermckenzie.com/sanctions-clauses-and-us-extraterritorial-sanctions-lamesa-v-cynergy-appeal/.

75. Royal Court of Justice, The Court of Appeal (Civil Division), Judgment, "Lamesa Investments Limited and Cynergy Bank Limited," June 30, 2020, https://www.judiciary.uk/wp-content/uploads/2020/07/Lamesa-v-Cynergy.APPROVED-JUDGMENTS.pdf.

76. Wilmer Hale, "Top EU Court Rules on the EU Blocking Regulation Against US Sanctions for the First Time," January 31, 2022, https://www.wilmerhale.com/insights/client-alerts/20220124-top-eu-court-rules-on-the-eu-blocking-regulation-against-us-sanctions-for-the-first-time.

77. OFAC, "Alfa Laval Middle East Ltd. Settles Potential Civil Liability for Apparent Violations of the Iranian Transactions and Sanctions Regulations," https://ofac.treasury.gov/media/911521/download?inline.

78. OFAC, "Stanley Black & Decker, Inc. Settles Potential Civil Liability for Apparent Violations of the Iranian Transactions and Sanctions Regulations Committed by its Chinese-Based Subsidiary Jiangsu Guoqiang Tools Co Ltd.," March 27, 2019, https://ofac.treasury.gov/media/13911/download?inline.

79. OFAC, "Guidance on the Provision of Certain Services Relating to the Requirements of US Sanctions Laws," January 12, 2017, https://ofac.treasury.gov/media/6211/download?inline.

80. OFAC, "OFAC Settles with Cameron International Corporation for Its Potential Civil Liability for Apparent Violations of Ukraine-Related Sanctions Regulations," September 27, 2021, https://ofac.treasury.gov/media/913321/download?inline.

81. OFAC, FAQ 12.

82. Department of the Treasury, "Treasury Announces $508 Million Settlement with British American Tobacco, Largest Ever Against Non-Financial Institution," April 25, 2023, https://home.treasury.gov/news/press-releases/jy1441.

83. Department of the Treasury, Enforcement Release, "OFAC Settles with Binance Holdings, Ltd. for $968,618,825 Related to Apparent Violations of Multiple Sanctions Programs," November 21, 2023, https://ofac.treasury.gov/media/932351/download?inline.

84. Department of Justice, Office of Public Affairs, Press Release, "US Citizen Who Conspired to Assist North Korea in Evading Sanctions Sentenced to Over Five Years and Fined $100,000," April 12, 2022, https://www.justice.gov/opa/pr/us-citizen-who-conspired-assist-north-korea-evading-sanctions-sentenced-over-five-years-and.

www.ingramcontent.com/pod-product-compliance
Lightning Source LLC
Chambersburg PA
CBHW062114040426
42337CB00042B/2468